THE BELIEF Principle

THE SEVEN BELIEFS THAT WILL
TRANSFORM YOUR LIFE

STEVEN AITCHISON

The Belief Principle: The Seven Beliefs That Will Transform Your Life

Published by CYT Media Ltd.

Steven Aitchison
www.TheBeliefPrinciple.com
author@thebeliefprinciple.com

Every attempt has been made to source all quotes correctly.

For additional copies or bulk purchases visit:
www.TheBeliefPrinciple.com

ISBN-10: 1838032703
ISBN-13: 978-1838032708

10 9 8 7 6 5 4 3 2 1

First Edition: 2019

Printed in the United States of America.

———

With the purchase this book, you also receive these bonuses in your membership area:

- Free MP3's
- Bonus chapters
- Mini-course on *The Belief Principle Affirmations*
- Exclusive access to Facebook and Telegram group
- Live Q & A with me

This book is dedicated to Sharon, Bradley, and Lewis who have supported me through every step of the entrepreneurial journey for the last 18 years. They frequently asked the question, "What is it that you actually do?"

Now my answer is much shorter, "I am a writer and online trainer."

Thank you for everything.

CONTENTS

PART 1: You And Your Beliefs

PART 2: Knowing The Beliefs You Have And Changing All The Rules

PART 3: The Deep Soul Feeling Method

PART 4: The Seven Beliefs That Will Transform Your Life

FOREWORD

Just how powerful are our beliefs?

If you decided to pick up this book, you must at least be curious, but listen to this...

I was born with a disease called Spinal Muscular Atrophy. It's similar to Lou Gehrig's disease (otherwise known as ALS), but it affects children. Most die before the age of two.

But not me. At the ripe old age of 37, not only am I still alive, but I've been blessed with a life many people only dream about.

I've lived on the beaches of Mexico, watched whales leaping through the surf off the coast of Canada, and explored the streets of Jerusalem, sometimes carried over the cobblestones by Israeli soldiers.

At home, I have a household staff of eight people.

They cook anything I desire, keep everything clean and tidy, and care for me 24 hours a day.

In business, I've become a multimillionaire, building an online magazine with millions of readers, tens of thousands of customers, and countless fans throughout the world.

And I did it all while sitting in a wheelchair, unable to move from the neck down.

Hard to believe?

If so, I don't blame you. I wouldn't believe it myself if I hadn't lived it.

But it's all true. I've built the life of my dreams with nothing more than my thoughts and words.

When they hear the story, many people ask, "How did you become so successful, despite your disability?"

The answer: I don't think of myself as disabled.

When I was a child, my mother actually never told me there was anything "wrong" with me. I didn't even hear the word "disabled" until I started kindergarten.

When I asked my mother what it meant, she told me, "It means you can't do something as well as someone else, but that's true for all of us. You might not be able to carry your books, but other children can't write as well as you can. The truth is, we are all disabled in some way."

It's an astonishing explanation, isn't it? But it's true, and it shaped the belief that nothing was wrong with me, that I was a human being with strengths and weaknesses like everyone else. By not thinking of myself as disabled, I lived as if I wasn't.

Since then, I've accumulated many empowering beliefs, and you'll find quite a few of those in this book. Steven has done a lovely job curating some of the most important beliefs you can instill within your mind, as well as giving you simple and clear advice on exactly how to do that.

If you let it, this book will help you remap your mind, change the way you see the world, and accomplish things the old you would have never thought possible. Not through "magic," but simply by shifting the way you think.

Embrace it. Do the exercises. Take the process seriously.

Your beliefs are more powerful than you could ever imagine. I'm living proof.

Jon Morrow
www.smartblogger.com

INTRODUCTION

How This Book Will Benefit You

With the help of this book, you are going to go on a journey. On this journey, you are going to discover a lot about yourself. You're going to find out beliefs held by you that are not even your own; some of them are literally hundreds of years old (you may be asking how that is possible, and I'll share that with you later on).

You are going to uncover seven beliefs that will quite literally change the course of your life forever, should you wish to install them. These seven beliefs are not the only beliefs that will change your life, as there are different beliefs for different areas of your life. However, if you install just these seven beliefs, or even a few of them, you will see a remarkable change happening over a period of weeks and months after you take action on the information in this book.

The Belief Principle

You'll also discover two words that you and every human being on the planet uses that are responsible for EVERYTHING you have ever achieved and failed at in your life.

Another big discovery you are going to make is something called *The Belief Ceiling* and the *Fiat Principle*, which is your beliefs surrounding money. Changing this one belief could literally change how much income you bring into your life as it has been holding you back from earning and attracting more money than you may previously have thought possible.

You will also learn that you have something called a *Belief Filter* which literally shapes how you see the world. Your version of the world is completely different from mine, and my version of the world is completely different from the other 7.8 billion people who reside on this planet and it's all to do with our belief filters.

You're going to learn what affirmations really are and how you have been using them unconsciously all of your life. The most exciting thing is you're going to learn how to use them consciously and change all the areas of your life you've always wanted to change.

Another huge discovery you'll make is the *Deep Soul Feeling Method*, which is a unique way to install new beliefs using a powerful mantra and an easy-to-follow process.

This book will help you set up the beliefs you need, and give you the tools you require, to become successful at whatever you put your mind to.

If you take action, here is what you can expect to gain from this book:

- Bring more money into your life.
- More happiness in all areas of your life.
- Renewed energy and hope that you really can create a life carved out by you.
- A high feeling of self worth.
- The freedom that comes from finding your purpose.
- Take back control of your life.
- Know, for certain, that you are capable of anything.
- You will find your inner courage.
- More joy.
- A drastic increase in confidence

- A new understanding of relationships and how to create stronger, empowering relationships in your life.
- Never, ever, ever settle for second best again.
- A sense of fulfilment.
- Increase your focus and concentration to get more things done.
- KNOW that you are enough.

Why I Wrote This Book

It was the punch in the mouth that got me thinking I was going to die. The boy holding me was just as crazy as the boy punching me, and although they were six and seven years old, they weren't the type of boys you wanted to mess with. Running through my young mind was the question why the two meanest school bullies in the world hated me so much, and I could only conclude it was because I was not very smart, or "thick" as we said back in the day.

Let me tell you why I thought I was getting bullied because I wasn't very smart, or I thought at the time I wasn't smart.

It started when I was around six years old while at primary school in a rough part of Edinburgh called Wester Hailes. I attended Clovenstone Primary School, and within a few years of being there, I started to feel there was something wrong with me, as I wasn't picking up the lessons as quickly as everyone else.

This steady decline was eventually flagged up to my parents when they attended parents' night and each teacher said that I was "slow to learn," my concentration wasn't good, my speech wasn't good, and my social interaction wasn't great, either. It was intimated that I had some kind of learning disability. Now, in my little head at that time, I naturally assumed I was "thick," not very PC, I know, however that's the word that swirled around my head at the time.

All the time, I was developing the belief that there was something wrong with me and I wasn't like the other children at school. This belief isolated me, and I learned to enjoy my own company and the company of my family.

It was discovered that I had something called "Glue Ear" which affected my ability to hear.

To fixit I had an operation to insert grommets into my ear.

After the operation, my learning ability picked up rapidly. What I had been doing for months was lip-reading. Far from being thick, I had learned to lip-read quite well, and the problems had occurred when the teachers had their backs to me or when I couldn't see their lips.

The school bullies were still there, however things started to get better after the operation on my ears.

One thing remained: my belief that I was thick stayed with me for years. I had developed the belief over time, and it had grown stronger the more evidence I'd found for it. I felt that everything I did was stupid, and I would magnify those feelings of stupidity in my mind.

There was nothing else to do but to declare to my young mind that I was just not intelligent and was never going to be.

This belief was carried with me throughout my young life and late into my teens. I found I revered intelligent people and always wondered how to "fix my brain" to become more intelligent. It affected me socially, too; I just didn't want to put myself in a situation where people would laugh at me, so I avoided social situations as much as I could.

How I Learned About Beliefs

The belief that "I am not intelligent" which had plagued me my whole life changed in one day.

I was walking home from school feeling pleased with myself for passing an exam in history. As I walked the mile to my home, I suddenly realized that I was intelligent. I told myself that if I can pass an exam in history, it must mean I had at least some degree of intelligence. My brain lit up. I started thinking about other pieces of evidence to prove I was intelligent: I loved reading, I liked writing stories, I had passed other exams, I had taken a keen interest in history, and a whole host of other signs.

In one day, I finally dropped the belief that I was not intelligent. From that day on, my interest in the human brain and psychology in particular was to change my life in so many ways.

The Belief Principle

As my new knowledge began to sink in, my confidence grew, and my proudest moment was being made vice-captain of my schoolhouse (Wemyss) when I was sixteen years old at Buckhaven High School— and what's more, I was nominated by one of the popular girls in school.

My newfound belief that "I am intelligent" helped me become the first person in my family to go to university. The degree course that I chose was psychology. What that degree did was show me just how our self-talk can either harm us psychologically or help us to grow. The degree cemented my love of the human mind and in particular the subject of personal beliefs.

My journey led me to discover that our whole lives are controlled by what we believe about ourselves, what we believe about the world, and what we believe about other people.

The amazing thing is that one belief that I held— "I am thick"– not only affected my view of myself as an intellectual being, it had an impact on every area of my life. It affected me socially, it affected my mental health, and it affected how I viewed the world around me.

That one belief literally changed the way I viewed the world in which I lived.

This new secret power of being able to change my limiting beliefs and install new empowering beliefs has led me to so many amazing things in my life:

- The first person in my family to attend university and gain a degree in psychology.
- Finding my perfect woman and being truly happy in my marriage.
- Started a business in 2004 and navigated the demise of that business.
- Started a new career in drug and alcohol counselling in 2006 which I loved for 6 years before moving on.
- Helped to raise two amazing boys to become men.
- Left my full-time job in 2012 to start a new business online in the personal development space.
- Created a successful Facebook page with over 3.7 million followers.
- Started a Facebook live show that brought in over 1 million viewers.
- Started another side business which made over $500,000 in sales over the course of 4 years.

- Started another side business trading and teaching cryptocurrency which is still running today.
- Wrote a phenomenally successful personal development book called *The Belief Principle* (Okay, maybe not. It's all a process so I believe I can make it phenomenally successful).

Okay, that's just some of the things I have achieved that I am willing to talk about and I believe, 100%, you can do anything you want to with the right beliefs.

You might wonder: How the hell do you change a belief? The better question to start with is: What beliefs do I hold about myself just now?

After my epiphany about beliefs, it didn't truly strike me just how important our beliefs are until I was older. Over the course of around twenty years, I managed to install new empowering beliefs in every single area of my life using a relatively simple formula.

The formula is so simple that other people will tell you that it can't be done. Trust me, it can be, and I'm going to show you how.

I have grasped one principle in life that can truly make a difference to millions of people around the world, and I think that is quite a discovery to talk about. I know that this message is going to take me down a long road, but the good thing is that it will survive me for hundreds of years to come. The principle is timeless.

I wanted to create a book that would not only help millions of people around the world, but also help many more millions in one hundred or two hundred years' time. My hope is that this book will be remembered and reused time and time again and passed down to different generations.

Is that an ego thing or is it something else? I like to think it is part of my purpose, however I recognize there will be an element of ego in there.

You see, I discovered that for personal development messages to survive the test of time, they must have two qualities:

Simplicity And Timelessness

We often mistake simplicity with how easy something is.

The Belief Principle

We all know that there's a very simple solution to losing weight: exercise more and eat less. That's an extremely simple solution but how hard is it to do in practice? So please do not dismiss the simplicity of the exercises in this book. They are simple principles yet extremely powerful.

The second is timelessness. This really pertains to what will be relevant tomorrow, what will be relevant 10 years from now, 50 years from now or even 200 years from now. A timeless book is one that will stand the test of time and it's not some fad.

This is precisely the reason that the new thought teachers of 100 years ago are starting to make a revival: James Allan, Neville Goddard, Charles Haanel, Napoleon Hill, Joseph Murphy, W. Clement Stone, Wallace Wattles, and Elizabeth Towne to name just a few.

Their thinking and thoughts are timeless and are still very much alive today.

However, their thoughts are really taken from principles and practices that have been swirling

12

around the minds of writers for hundreds of years previously.

I have attempted to make this book timeless so that if someone finds a copy buried somewhere in 500 years' time it will still be useful and relevant.

For change to happen in our life we need to take action and I would love your very first action to be joining our Facebook group at: *www.TheBeliefPrinciple.com/FBGroup*.

Here, you will find people who are on a similar path to you who practice positive living. When you purchase the book you will also get access to the exclusive group groups with more resources to help you on your journey.

Okay, time to get going…

As Cipher said to Neo in the *The Matrix (1999)*, "Buckle your seatbelt, Dorothy, 'cause Kansas is going bye-bye."

The Belief Principle

PART 1

———

YOU AND YOUR BELIEFS

CHAPTER 1

Change Is Easy

"You have the chance every single morning to make that change and be the person you want to be."

BRENDON BURCHARD

This is extremely important to understand and is one statement that can be the difference between succeeding in life and not succeeding, so I really need you to see how important it is.

Seriously, if you mentally skip over this, you will hinder your progress in life drastically.

Okay, I think you now know how important this is.

I would like you to repeat over and over in your head as much as possible for the next few days:

The Belief Principle

"Changing my beliefs is easy and fun."

One of the biggest lies we unconsciously tell ourselves is that change is hard, life is hard, relationships are hard, and doing something new is hard; it's all too difficult. With this frame of mind, we never get anything done. We don't take the first step, and we forget about our dreams, our goals, and our ambitions in life. You deserve an amazing life, you deserve money, love, a great job, and that amazing feeling of happiness.

When you change this one belief, it is going to change your life so fundamentally you're going to wish you had worked on your belief's years ago.

Normally when we are driving, waiting in line, at work, daydreaming, or idly thinking about things, we repeat the same thoughts over and over and over again, which is why we are stuck where we are, unable to get what we want in life. To change something in your life means you have to change something. That sounds obvious, right?

But it has been a revelation for a lot of people.

So for the next few days, I would like you to experience being mindful, and whenever you get a experience being mindful, and whenever you get a spare moment to think (that's a big chunk of your day), I would like you to repeat:

"Changing my beliefs is easy and fun."
  "Changing my beliefs is easy and fun."
    "Changing my beliefs is easy and fun."
      "Changing my beliefs is easy and fun."
        "Changing my beliefs is easy and fun."

There is a lot more to changing a belief than reciting an affirmation over and over, of course, and depending on the belief, some are much easier to install than others. I call these types of beliefs leaf beliefs, which you'll learn more about.

This one belief, "Changing my beliefs is easy and fun," will not have a lot of opposition in your mind, which is why I chose that particular affirmation. A new belief that has a lot of opposition in your mind is called cognitive dissonance, and it tends to happen in root beliefs and trunk beliefs.

I will give you the tools in this book to make

changing your root and trunk beliefs even easier, but for now, I want you to experience the first part of your journey, and it's a journey we, as a community, will be taking together.

You are going to be part of the #BeliefPrinciple community. So whenever you talk about this on social media, use the hashtag #BeliefPrinciple so we can quickly search and find our community on all platforms.

Do you need to become a part of the community? Certainly not. But studies have shown that belonging to a community, even if it is online, makes change much easier than going it alone. Still, this is entirely your decision.

There is a Telegram and Facebook group that accompanies this book, which you can join here:

Telegram: *www.TheBeliefPrinciple.com/telegram*
Facebook: *www.TheBeliefPrinciple.com/group*

There is also a resources section that you can access and will give you additional downloads and training to accompany this book:
www.TheBeliefPrinciple/resources

Change Is Easy

C H A P T E R   S U M M A R Y

———

- Installing the new belief, "Change is easy" will help us to take the first steps in anything new we want to try.

- Repeat the affirmation "Changing my beliefs is easy and fun" whenever you get the chance.

- A new belief that has a lot of opposition in your mind is called cognitive dissonance.

- Use the hashtags #BeliefPrinciple, #BeliefBuster, or #BeliefCreator whenever you use social media to talk about this book.

The Belief Principle

CHAPTER 2

What Are Beliefs?

"I was exhilarated by the new realization that I could change the character of my life by changing my beliefs. I was instantly energized because I realized that there was a science-based path that would take me from my job as a perennial 'victim' to my new position as 'co-creator' of my destiny."

BRUCE H. LIPTON, Ph.D.

What Is A Belief?

The *Oxford English Dictionary* defines belief as:

"Something one accepts as true or real; a firmly held opinion."

You will notice that all definitions of belief, when it pertains to personal beliefs, talk about them from a subjective point of view.

23

The Intangible Soup Of Nothingness

Your mind is literally a collection of beliefs, thoughts, memories and ideas that swirl around in your head on a daily basis. This intangible soup of nothingness in your mind is the foundation of your life.

That sounds crazy when you hear it like that. We cannot touch, feel, see, hear or taste our beliefs and yet they control everything we do from going to work every day to the people we choose to have in our lives, to how much money we make or how successful we are going to be.

If something is made of nothing, how then can it be responsible for the very life we are currently leading and more to the point, how do we change it to live a better life?

That's the big question.

Once you realize just how beliefs are formed, you will then be able to grasp just how easy and fun it's going to be to work on each of your limiting beliefs.

Beliefs Are Subjective

What does that mean? Well, basically it means that a personal belief is true for you but not necessarily true for everyone else. I like this quote from Elle Sommer, a dear friend of mine:

> "Your beliefs don't even have to be true; they don't even have to be close to the truth, e.g., superstitions, prejudices, but they still mold the outer world with the inner arrangements of our minds."

For example, you might absolutely believe that you will never be able to lose weight, while one thousand other people will tell you that they know otherwise. However, because you believe that statement, your body will respond in kind and help you NOT to lose weight.

That's a shocker, isn't it? What you tell yourself, you are really communicating to your body, as well.

Dr. Joe Dispenza, in his book *You Are the Placebo: Making Your Mind Matter*, states:

"Are we more likely to suffer from arthritis, stiff joints, poor memory, flagging energy, and decreased sex drive as we age, simply because that's the version of the truth that ads, commercials, television shows, and media reports bombard us with? What other self-fulfilling prophecies are we creating in our minds without being aware of what we're doing? And what 'inevitable truths' can we successfully reverse simply through thinking new thoughts and choosing new beliefs?"

The truth is what you tell yourself is true, what you tell your body is true, what you tell your mind is true, but where does the truth come from?

Where Does The Truth Come From?

It has everything to do with our conscious and subconscious mind and how we talk to ourselves.

We feed the subconscious mind with ideas that are, at best, half-formed, and the subconscious mind tries to prove what your conscious mind has told it.

In a study in 2002 reported in the *Journal of Personality and Social Psychology* by Levy et al., it was found that people over the age of fifty who had more positive beliefs about aging lived, on average, 7.5 years longer than people with negative beliefs about ageing. Nearly eight years longer!!

That is the power of the mind. What has to happen for one to live an extra 7.5 years?

Obviously, lots of things are going on in the body and the mind, but it shows a clear correlation between the two.

When I research findings like this, it still amazes me to think that we don't take care of what we put into our minds on a daily basis. This is why monitoring our beliefs is so important; it's not all woo-woo and positivity—it genuinely makes a huge difference in your life.

A Billion-Dollar Belief

In 2012, driven by a deep belief of transparency and fairness in the stock markets, Rob Park, Brad Katsuyama, and Ronan Ryan went about setting up their own stock exchange.

The Belief Principle

While working at the Royal Bank of Canada (RBC), the global electronic trading team led by Brad Katsuyama, Ronan Ryan, John Schwall, and Rob Park discovered that the stock exchanges were enabling predatory trading strategies that were harming long-term investors representing the savings of millions of people.

Michael Lewis, author of *Flash Boys* which describes the investigation into the phenomenon of high-frequency trading (HFT) in the U.S. equity market, interviewed and collected the experiences of several individuals working on Wall Street.

Lewis concludes that HFT is used as a method to front run orders placed by investors. He goes further to suggest that broad technological changes and unethical trading practices have transformed the U.S. stock market from "the world's most public, most democratic, financial market" into a "rigged" market. This was high speed trading.

The view that Michael Lewis had was the same view that Brad Katsuyama had, only Brad and his team wanted to do something about it.

Ultimately, the team decided that the best way to change the system was to build a new exchange from scratch that would put the interests of investors first: The Investors Exchange (IEX) was born.

Brad Katsuyama and his team wanted to change the "rigged market" and make it a fair market for everyone, but it would take time, money and a lot of effort to get there.

Driven by their belief in a fairer stock exchange, the team's Investors Exchange (IEX) debuted as an Alternative Trading System in 2013, and the IEX was launched as a national stock exchange for U.S. equities in 2016.

Since its introduction, IEX has developed and introduced innovations that aim to level the playing field and offer superior performance for all market participants, whether that's through IEX's "speed bump," which is designed to ensure that the exchange executes trades at the right price, or the IEX Signal (i.e., Crumbling Quote Indicator), a machine learning-based signal that aims to protect investors from trading while prices are unstable.

That belief of injustice drove Brad Katsuyama and his colleagues to change something about the system. Although it was an internal belief about injustice and the need to do something about it, there was so much more to what Katsuyama did here.

He had to change his belief about having the power to do something about it.

Katsuyama was not a tech guy at all and didn't know the first thing about starting an exchange, but his self-belief and his belief of injustice drove him to give up his well-paid job and go out and start a brand-new stock exchange.

IEX now regularly trades billions of dollars worth of shares every single day and does it in a much fairer way than all other exchanges. This was made possible with the power of belief.

Taking Responsibility

Brad Katsuyama knew there was something wrong with the system and had a root belief about justice, but he took responsibility for this and did something about it.

There is no getting away from the fact that we have to take responsibility for our own direction in life and in all areas of our lives.

There are many more studies that tell us that what we believe will affect our health, our wealth, our goals, our relationships, our spirituality, and even our mortality. So now it's time to sit up and take notice and ask yourself what mental junk has been stored in your brain for too long and is harming you.

There is a power that comes from taking responsibility for every aspect of our lives, and it's something we MUST do in order to take charge of the direction our lives are taking.

Locus Of Control

In his 1977 paper, "Self-Efficacy: Toward a Unifying Theory of Behavioral Change," Albert Bandura talks about locus of control.

Locus of control is the degree to which people believe that they have control over the outcome of events in their lives, as opposed to external forces beyond their control.

Understanding of the concept was developed by Julian B. Rotter in 1954 and has since become an aspect of personality studies.

Effectively, there is a scale for the locus of control from a high internal locus of control to a high external locus of control. Internal locus of control is when we believe we have control, to a large extent, over what happens to us in life.

For example, if I am overweight, I believe I have the power to control my weight by taking steps to stop putting on more weight and starting to lose weight, e.g., exercise, eating less, etc.

External locus of control is when we blame external factors for various situations in life. Again, going back to the overweight example, a lot of people will say things like, "I eat too much because I am stressed about work," "I don't have time to exercise," and "The kids need my attention more."

By taking responsibility for everything in our lives, from our relationships to the jobs we have, we will have a much higher internal locus of control.

This allows us to change our beliefs much quicker than someone who tends to blame external factors on what happens to them in life.

Think About

Take a moment now to think about the various areas of your life and think about the degree to which you blame external factors for your situation (internal locus of control)?

Examples of this could be your current job, your relationships, your wealth, your health, your social life, etc.

The quick exercise above might be an eye-opener for you, as most of us automatically have a subconscious preference when it comes to the locus of control. Take your time with this exercise and really dig deep.

I will talk about ways to have a much higher internal locus of control, and it will come naturally when you start to work on your beliefs; however, I would like you to bring your locus of control into your conscious mind rather than letting it stay stuck in your subconscious.

This way, you will immediately have a degree of control over it simply by being aware.

Become conscious of the fact that changes are coming to your life and start to get excited about that—it's all down to YOU.

Next, we are going to look at where your beliefs come from and how some of your beliefs are literally hundreds of years old.

What Are Beliefs?

CHAPTER SUMMARY

- A belief is: "Something one accepts as true or real; a firmly opinion."

- Your beliefs are completely subjective.

- Your truth is whatever you feed your mind at any given time.

- The Billion Dollar Belief is about Brad Katsuyama and how his belief about the stock markets being unfair led him to start a billion-dollar company.

- Locus of control is the degree to which people believe that they have control over the outcome of events in their lives, as opposed to external forces beyond their control.

- Think about: Take a moment to think about the various areas of your life and about the degree to which you blame external factors for your situation.

The Belief Principle

CHAPTER 3

The Etiology Of A Belief

"Faith is a place of mystery, where we find the courage to believe in what we cannot see and the strength to let go of our fear of uncertainty."

BRENÉ BROWN

You Are What You Believe You Are!

The path you are walking in life right now has been determined by the beliefs you have subconsciously installed in your mind. Think about that for a few seconds and let me ask you a question:

What are you good at?

Take a moment to answer. Focus on ONE thing you are really good at.

It could be work-related, a skill you have, a way of dealing with people, a hobby—just name one thing you are good at.

Got one? Good.

Now think about where the belief that you are good at (insert what you are good at here) came from.

I don't know what you said you were good at, but chances are what you said will follow a similar path to this belief. When I asked someone this question at a talk, here is roughly how the conversation went:

Q: What one thing are you good at?
A: (After a little bit of thought) I am good at researching and writing research papers.

Q: When did you realize you were good at researching?
A: When I started university.

Q: And how did you discover you were good
at   researching?
A: When I started writing my research papers, I was always good at finding the

right information and data to put into my essays and putting my papers in the right structure that was required. Then my lecturers started commenting about my research papers, and I always received high marks, and my friends in the course started asking me how I do it.

Q: So, were there specific phrases that people used when they praised you?

A: It was more the questions they asked, like "How did you find that information," "Where did you go to get that data?," and "Where did you learn to do your research papers like that?"

Q: And what did that tell you about your research skills?

A: Well, it told me I must be good, otherwise I wouldn't get so many comments, and my marks for the research papers I wrote were always high. If it were only a few comments, I would have dismissed it, but it was a lot of people who asked me about researching.

Q: Did you tell anybody your methodology for doing research and writing research papers?

A: I did actually. I wrote a 3-page guide for a few of my classmates (She laughed). It was passed around to a lot of other students at university.

Q: So you now believe you are good at researching and writing research essays?

A: Definitely.

Q: When did you finish university?

A: I am still there in my fourth year.

That conversation is typical of how a lot of beliefs are formed in adulthood, and if we break it down, we will find the formula for how a belief is formed:

- **Perception.** I am good at researching and writing research papers.

- **Evidence.** High marks on my papers. "How did you find that information." "Where did you go to get that data?" "Where did you learn to do your research papers like that?" Then my lecturers started commenting about my research papers.

- **Repetition.** Continuous feedback on research papers and writing skills from lecturers and classmates.

- **Time.** This is ongoing, so this belief has been firmly planted and grown over the space of three years.

We will talk in much more depth about this belief formula, as there can be other factors involved, but that is the crux of how a belief is formed.

The Tree Of Beliefs

One belief tends to grow branches and touch other areas of our lives. Think about the effect that the belief of being good at researching and writing research papers will have in other areas of this woman's life:

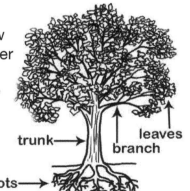

- Confidence to write.
- Confidence in her general abilities to do well at university.

- Good organizational skills.
- Good at communicating with her classmates.
- Communicating her process to other classmates.
- Communicating with her lecturers.
- Ability to speak in public.
- The confidence to try other things in life because of the positive reactions to her researching and writing ability.
- General self-esteem.

I could write another hundred branch beliefs from that one belief. This shows that one belief does not occur on its own; there is a network effect of beliefs that are all intertwined, and I call it *The Tree of Beliefs*.

Now, think about someone who had extremely low self-confidence, had been told they were worthless most of their life, and always shied away from any kind of praise. If they had been told the same things as the university student, they wouldn't have accepted the initial perception that they were good at researching and writing research papers. That belief would not have been installed into the mind of someone who had clashing beliefs about themselves.

This is further evidence of the network effect at work.

This is why we have to look at *The Tree of Beliefs* and work on some of the main fundamental beliefs we have about ourselves. We have four different types of beliefs about ourselves:

1. **Root beliefs.**
2. **Trunk beliefs.**
3. **Branch beliefs.**
4. **Leaf beliefs.**

Bear in mind that we are not talking about world beliefs here, or religious beliefs, or anything outside of yourself. This is purely the beliefs you hold about yourself.

The tree analogy does not work on world beliefs, as there is a tribal mentality in world beliefs that would fall under a forest belief effect if we were to keep the tree analogy alive.

1. Root Beliefs

These are your core beliefs and can be difficult to change. For example, your religious beliefs.

These beliefs have been formed and molded since you were born, and they create the bedrock of who you are. They can be changed when something dramatic happens, but it is rare.

2. Trunk Beliefs

These are not as deep-set as your root beliefs and can be changed with some evidence and personal experience. For example, when you say, "I am not an intelligent person" and you firmly believe this, well, that belief can be changed with some work. It is mainly the trunk beliefs that we will be working with, which will feed some of your root beliefs also.

3. Branch Beliefs

These are smaller beliefs that have an impact on your life but not as much as a root or trunk belief. An example of this might be when you say to someone, "I don't enjoy reading books."

It could be true, but it could also be true that you've just never picked up the right book to enjoy or found the time to find a genre you love.

4. Leaf Beliefs

These beliefs are insignificant in and of themselves, but we have to be careful and not form a cluster of limiting leaf beliefs, which could lead to a more permanent belief being formed. An example of this might be, "I don't particularly like flying," which may be true, and this belief has no real impact on your life.

Other cluster beliefs might lead you to develop an irrational fear of flying, which might make you avoid travel and in turn have an impact on seeing family, going abroad with your loved ones, or taking trips with friends. Leaf beliefs might seem insignificant, but we still have to pay attention to them.

Now, something we have to take note of here is the fact that your root beliefs can affect the whole tree: the trunk, branch, and leaf beliefs.

Think about this scenario for a second: you were once a deeply religious person, and that was at the core of who you were. Then, something happened to totally rock your world, and you instantly lost faith in religion altogether.

This situation not only affects your faith and your religious beliefs, but it will have a huge impact on your outlook on life, your self-esteem, your positivity, your amenability, your openness, and your friendliness—you get where I am going with this. It will literally affect almost every other belief you have about yourself and the world around you.

Again, this is part of the network effect we spoke about earlier. This is why it is so important to know your root and trunk beliefs—they affect every other belief you have.

CHAPTER SUMMARY

———

- You are what you believe you are. Think of something you're good at and try to find out why you believe you are good at that particular thing.

- A simple story to illustrate how a belief is formed.

- *The Tree of Beliefs* is the network effect that our beliefs have on our whole life.

The Belief Principle

CHAPTER 4

Where Do We Get Our Beliefs?

"Every belief has a consequence. Long term, your beliefs determine your destiny."

MARIE FORLEO

We've just seen an example of how our beliefs can be formed when we are older. In general, though, our beliefs about ourselves and the world around us are formed at a much younger age.

Psychologists suggest that most of our beliefs have already been formed by the age of seven.

Seven Years Old!

We are not cognitively able to comprehend what beliefs are at that age and have not yet that will affect our lives at such a young age? Well, it's fully formed our own views of the world, and yet most of our beliefs about the world are already created, and we carry them on into adulthood. So where do the beliefs come from?

Most of our beliefs come from our teachers, our peers, our close family, and TV and media, and, predominantly, our parents or the people who raised us as children.

You've got to ask yourself: If your parents are the primary source of your beliefs, where did they get their beliefs from? Well, they got them from their parents, and their parents got them from their parents.

So in effect, some of your beliefs are literally hundreds of years old, passed down from generation to generation.

That's not to say that's a bad thing, as some beliefs stand us in good stead, e.g., believing that family is important, you have to work hard to get somewhere in life, you should believe in justice, all people should be treated with respect, and so on.

So why, then, are we designed to form beliefs partly to do with our brain biology and partly to do with the way we are brought up—nature and nurture.

As a species we grow by evolving, and evolution takes place over millions of years. However, if our previous generations keep on passing down information that helps us to form beliefs that will hold us back in life, we are not going to evolve very quickly as a human race.

Thank goodness we have evolved so much that we have access to information at our fingertips.

Socioeconomic Belief Divide

A few hundred years ago, we wouldn't have had access to all the amazing minds we have access to on a daily basis due to social media and the Internet. There is no doubt we are living in an information age and that we are starting to level the playing field when it comes to our own economic status.

What the information age has done is allow us to try on different theories to see what works for us as individuals.

Freud And Jung

Freud and Jung built up a large following in their time through word of mouth, but the trouble was that word of mouth is a slow process.

It was the upper classes who had access to Freud's theories, and they were very much a minority, but due to their influence on society, what they believed was passed on to the masses.

Then Jung comes along and says, "Freud! He's talking mince. Here is what I believe." And so it was that the younger generation of the upper class started following Jung, making him the new "man of the hour," and again the upper classes belief in Jung was passed down to the masses.

Today, with our greater access to information and research tools, we are far more willing to try different theories in all areas of our lives.

This is the reason YouTube, Facebook, Twitter, TikTok, and Instagram are so popular—we now have the opportunity to join a tribe of people who are walking the same path as us.

A Little Bit About Brainwaves

Our brains generate electrical signals or brainwaves, which can be measured by an electroencephalograph (EEG). Brainwaves are divided into four predominant speed ranges or patterns, each of which played a critical role in our mental development during our childhood. And today, they play an important role in maintaining our health and vitality as adults. Your brain can be functioning in more than one brainwave state concurrently; however, there are specific times when each state will dominate.

As adults, we mostly function in the beta brainwave state, which is the normal tick-tock world of ordinary day-to-day things in life, like taking care of bills, working, or watching TV, but when we sleep, we go through all of the brainwave states in order to help our bodies and minds rest and recuperate.

Our programming years are between birth and age seven. During these years, our children will spend most of their time in alpha and theta brainwave cycles, which occur during hypnosis or meditation.

53

So you may want to imagine your little children walking around in a permanent state of hypnosis, being programmed by the environment, open to suggestions, in a super learning state.

These are the years when we take on beliefs about ourselves and life, and many of these will remain unconscious throughout the rest of our lives, though they will show up in our behaviors, our achievements, our goals, how we choose our friends, our life partners, and so on.

If you think about it, every belief that you have has been put there or suggested by somebody else.

So, as you can see from the above, a crucial time in helping our children install positive beliefs about themselves is from birth to age seven. What would we like them to believe about themselves and life in general?

This is the time to instill positive messages, as they will be accepted as true. Comments like, "Your sister is smarter than you," "You are so clumsy," or "Big boys don't cry," will have a huge impact.

One of the biggest tools that you can give them is a powerful, positive, and healthy belief system. The most limiting beliefs that I see turning up with my clients in later years, time and time again, are those like, "I'm not good enough," "I'm not deserving," "I'm worthless," and "I am unlovable."

These beliefs have been installed, typically, before the age of seven and in most cases unintentionally by well-meaning parents.

Having this knowledge of brainwaves means we are beginning to understand how the beliefs we have work. Essentially, we are looking at how we have been programmed and how we can reprogram ourselves. On another level, we can also use this knowledge to help our children become more balanced individuals later in life.

CHAPTER SUMMARY

———

- Most of the beliefs we hold have been formed by the age of seven.

- The Socioeconomic Belief Divide has been narrowed due to information, once reserved for the wealthy, that we ALL have at our fingertips now.

- Our brainwave patterns contribute to the beliefs we have installed at an early age, which was predominantly in the theta-alpha range. Whereas, as adults, we are in a beta brainwave state which is not conducive to learning and changing beliefs.

CHAPTER 5

The Filter Bubble

"When life gets stressful, we focus often on what we've failed at, or what we've not accomplished, or the mistakes we've made. We tend to forget all the things that we've done really well. So this is the time to ignore the failures and think of the wins."

DEAN GRAZIOSI

You've dragged yourself out of bed, had your shower, brushed your teeth, and it's time to sit and relax before you head out to work. You grab a cup of coffee and scroll through your news feed and favorite websites. You're skimming the news feeds and bookmarking some of your favorite articles to read later.

You like a few posts on Facebook, share a few funny videos with friends, and read a few articles.

All seems fairly harmless, doesn't it? Only it's not—you are being tracked, and you are being shown more of the information that you read on a daily basis. How harmful can that be? Well, you are being put into a "filter bubble," a term coined by Internet activist Eli Pariser.

What Is A Filter Bubble?

In his book, *The Filter Bubble: What the Internet Is Hiding From You*, Pariser is saying that depending on what you search, where you search and what you click on after you have searched for something on the Internet, you will be shown more of the same kinds of information the next time you go to search for something.

The filter bubble is fascinating from a number of different viewpoints, and so is the term "echo chamber." An echo chamber is a metaphorical description to describe how our beliefs may be strengthened by the repetition of communication inside a closed system such as social media. (Barberá, Pablo, et al., "Tweeting from left to right: Is online political communication more than an echo chamber?" *Psychological Science* 26.10 (2015): 1531-1542.)

For example, if you are searching the term "Boris Johnston" and clicking on positive articles about Boris Johnston, the algorithm of that particular platform will show you more and more positive articles about Boris Johnston, therefore amplifying your positive view due to the fact that the platform algorithm is not showing you a more balanced view. This is the echo chamber.

So what the hell does this have to do with beliefs?

Well, we have a similar filter bubble in our mind, which can strengthen the beliefs that we have about ourselves.

Think of your mind just now as an Internet of thoughts. You have millions of thoughts in your lifetime, but you don't act on 99.99% of them. When you have a thought about yourself, it's usually in the form of a perception: "I look good today," "I feel great," or "I am feeling amazing."

When you have one of these thoughts, your mind immediately goes to work to try and prove your perception is correct, so it will look for other things in your life that support the perception, for example, that you feel amazing about life:

Your work is going well, your financial situation is good, your relationships with friends are good, and you feel healthy. All those things form part of the filter bubble.

Your mind is filtering out anything that could go against feeling amazing, e.g., your car broke down, your house is untidy, or one of the kids is not doing so well at school. So just like the filter bubble on social media, our minds have a filter bubble.

Unfortunately, the filter bubble doesn't tend to work when we are filtering out "bad" things in our life—it usually works the other way around and filters out the good things, the things we should feel truly grateful for.

So your mind is the thinker, and your subconscious acts like a prover.

The Thinker And The Prover

In his book, *Prometheus Rising*, Robert Anton Wilson describes our conscious and subconscious minds perfectly:

> "As Dr. Leonard Orr has noted, the human mind behaves as if it were divided into two parts, the Thinker and the Prover."

The Thinker can think about virtually anything. The Prover is a much simpler mechanism. It operates on one law only: "Whatever the Thinker thinks, the Prover proves."

Confirmation Bias

What Leonard Orr and Robert Anton Wilson were saying is what is known as confirmation bias. Basically, it operates like this:

You tell yourself something about yourself, e.g., *I am no good with technology*. That's the conscious mind (The Thinker). The subconscious mind (The Prover) then has to prove that what you are saying is true, so it looks for evidence.

The prover will think about all the examples of when you have not been good with technology: That time you touched a keyboard and the computer blew up, the time you hovered over a button on the screen and the whole website shut down, or the time you tried to send an embarrassing photo to your friend and you accidentally sent it to everyone on your contact list.

Obviously, these examples are exaggerated, which is what we do when we tell stories to other people, but you get the picture.

Your subconscious mind, the prover, gets to work on anything that the thinker says.

Take a moment to think about what you, the thinker, tell yourself, and see if any of these examples are true for you:

- "I am no good with computers."
- "I am terrible in social situations."
- "I always attract the wrong men."
- "I am never going to find love."
- "I could never afford that."
- "I could never write a book."
- "She'll never date someone like me."
- "I don't have the confidence to do that."
- "I've got a shitty life."
- "I don't deserve to be loved."
- "I am not worthy."

- "I'll never be wealthy."

When you say something like the statements above, your subconscious mind will take a statement and find evidence to prove it and shut down the parts of the mind that would have otherwise found evidence to the contrary.

So, if you're a man or a woman who says, "I always attract the wrong men," you're basically telling your subconscious mind to look out for the men who are going to be wrong for you, which is why you continue to attract the idiots that treat you like shit.

Telling yourself that will also have the knock-on effect of lowering your self esteem, lowering your feeling of self worth and generally depleting your self confidence. When you have extreme low self confidence you will accept love from people you wouldn't normally give the time of day.

The Three-Word Affirmation

Have you ever gone into a shop and bought an expensive piece of clothing, and then the minute you get out of the shop you get buyer's remorse? I would say, in general, a lot of women have done this. Why does this happen?

Again, it's all to do with confirmation bias.

You see a beautiful dress, you get excited and say, "Oh my god, that is beautiful."

You then imagine yourself wearing it and imagine where you will be when you're wearing it. You hear all the amazing comments from your friends. You try it on, and joy of joys, your bum actually looks good in it. That's it, you look at the price tag and think, "Screw it!" and you purchase it.

Confirmation bias all the way—you've convinced yourself you'll look great, you'll feel great, other people will admire you, your bum looks amazing in it, and it's totally worth it.

Then the minute you get out the shop door, you start another form of confirmation bias: "Oh, the kids need new school clothes, we're saving for a holiday, we need a new cooker, as well, the funds are actually running a bit low, and the dress is a bit pricey," and you convince yourself to take the dress back.

You buy with your emotions and return with your logic, all using confirmation bias.

My wife used to go through the same process whenever she would shop. She always had buyer's remorse and returned a lot of the clothes she bought. The way I helped her to stop buyer's remorse was simply helping her to install a new belief with a three-word affirmation:

"You deserve it."

Those three little words over the years have helped my wife get rid of buyer's remorse, and trust me, there's no one more deserving than my wife. She still occasionally reverts to form and gets the odd pang of regret but on the whole is recovering from buyer's remorse syndrome.

Buyer's remorse is similar to what we do in our own minds but over a much longer period of time.

The way we install a limiting belief is exactly the same way we install an empowering belief. I'll give you the exact formula later on, but three components are time, evidence, and repetition.

When you tell yourself something, you are really instructing your subconscious mind to look for evidence that what you say is true, and because you tell yourself something over a long period of time and have gathered lots of evidence to prove it, it becomes a belief—limiting or empowering.

Do you think you should have a good life? Do you think you should have great relationships? Do you think you should be wealthy? Do you think you should have a great career? I want to tell you something just now before we go on:

You Deserve It

I want to show you how to get your conscious and subconscious mind to work together, to work for you, to start receiving the things you do want in life. It's going to seem like magic, and that's because it is—if you define magic as something out of the ordinary.

With this in mind, can you see why a lot of the beliefs you hold about yourself could be wrong?

I hope you can. If you know your beliefs are subjective and accept that you can sometimes be wrong about your beliefs, and you now know all about confirmation bias, then you have to accept that the limiting beliefs you currently hold about yourself may be wrong, as well.

CHAPTER SUMMARY

- A filter bubble is when we subconsciously look for information to support the beliefs we have about ourselves.

- Leonard Orr spoke about the Thinker and the Prover which is effectively what the filter bubble is.

- Confirmation bias is when someone looks for evidence to support their hypothesis.

- The three-word affirmation: "You deserve it."

CHAPTER 6

The Power Of Beliefs

*"Beliefs are choices. First you choose your beliefs.
Then your beliefs affect your choices."*

ROY T. BENNETT

Potatoes have been a staple of our diet for the last few hundred years. However, the history of the potato suggests it has not had an easy ride. (Bear with me here, there's a point to this).

The story of the potato explains how the Spanish Conquistadors, who, after a trip to Peru in 1532, brought the potato, originally called batata (sweet potato), into Europe. It was then mispronounced by the Europeans and called potato.

A few Spanish farmers began cultivating it with the intention of giving it to their livestock as feed.

Knowledge of the potato spread across Europe very slowly until the 1600's when it was known all over Europe.

The potato was viewed with suspicion; the general opinion was that it wasn't fit for human consumption. However, the upper classes saw the potential of the potato, mainly to be able to feed the nation very cheaply.

During the revolutionary wars in the 1700's, the potato really took off as a dietary staple because there was a shortage of food, but still, it was regarded with distaste.

Peasants were still suspicious of the potato even after the Paris Faculty of Medicine testified in 1771 that the potato was not harmful to humans but in fact beneficial.

The great part of this story is that Fredrick the Great of Prussia had wanted to feed his nation with potatoes, but because his peasants regarded them with distaste, there was a resistance to grow them—there were even a few recorded cases of farmers being hanged for refusing to cultivate potatoes.

So Fredrick the Great thought about this and knew he would have to change how the potato was perceived, which he did by growing potatoes in his royal field. He "heavily" armed the field with guards—a show for the peasants.

Because the field was guarded, the people associated it with something worth stealing. Soon, peasants started to steal and eat the potatoes. Thus, the perception of the potato was changed forever, and it was cultivated widely throughout the world. This was down to the fact that Frederick the Great had changed the perception of the potato—the beliefs about the potato—using reverse psychology and had essentially tricked the peasants into thinking it was a royal food.

This is exactly what happens within our minds. We are brought up with other people's perceptions of life. Not until we develop enough intellectually can we change those perceptions, and even then, it can be difficult.

Until a perception is questioned in someone's mind, a belief cannot be changed; therefore, to start the process of installing a new belief or changing an old, limiting belief, a perception

Must first be challenged. Like the above story illustrates, the perception at the time was that potatoes weren't fit for a dog.

Frederick the Great did an amazing job at altering the perception of the potato, but he did something more important—he proved it was possible to get people to change their perception purely by reframing the potato in a different way.

You are going to do the same—no, not change your perception of the potato, but change some of the perceptions you have about yourself.

The Circular Compound Effect

When you change one belief, the starter belief, it automatically has a knock-on effect for other beliefs in your life, which have a knock-on effect on smaller beliefs. All this comes full circle and boosts the original belief, the starter belief, even more.

Imagine for a few seconds that you are extremely confident—not arrogant, rude, or egotistical; you are just very self-assured and truly believe in yourself.

How do you think this would change the way you are as a person? What opportunities would it open up? What do your social interactions look like? What jobs would you be willing to go for? Would you carry yourself differently?

The root belief of confidence is one belief that has a major impact on a lot of other beliefs, large and small, and it all compounds to give you even more confidence.

Here's a perfect example:

When I was in my teens, I was awkwardly shy in social situations and terrible when it came to talking to girls. If you've ever cringed as you watched a social interaction between two people obviously having an awkward time of it, then you understand what I was like all the time in social situations.

I always had the false notion that I had to speak more, or I had to be funny, or I had to have swagger.

Everybody used to always say, "You don't say much, do you?"

That would lead tome trying to force myself to talk to people and trying to tell stories when I wasn't really interested in talking or, in some cases, the people I was talking to, and it would lead to that cringe factor.

Later on, I realized three things:

1. **You only need one good story or anecdote for people to remember you.**
2. **For people to think you are good at socializing, all you need to do is ask everyone lots of questions about themselves.**
3. **Being a quiet person gets people interested in you.**

Point number one. I am not a good story collector or teller, and I quickly forget a lot of the good stories that have happened in my life. My younger sister, Izzy, is brilliant at stories, and she is hilarious because she remembers everything.

So, realizing this, I would collect stories in my head and rehearse them and try to use them as much as possible so I could remember them for social situations.

Then when I was at a social gathering, I could bring up one story, and for about one minute, all the attention was on me, and people would remember my story and actually see me as a genuinely interesting person. I might have been in a crowd of people for four hours, and that one minute was enough for people to think of me as quite chatty and confident.

Point number two. Most people love to talk about themselves and knowing this is fantastic because if you're really shy, all you have to do is listen to people and ask them questions where appropriate, e.g., "Oh, you work at such and such. How do you like it?"

One trick here is to ask open-ended questions rather than questions with yes or no answers.

If you move around the people in the gathering like this, they will remember you as really friendly and warm, as most people don't take a genuine interest.

This also has the effect of building up your confidence in social situations, which has a compounding effect of higher self-esteem, a feeling of higher self-worth, the confidence to try new things, and an overall feeling of deep self-belief.

Point number three. I quickly discovered I became more interesting to girls when I was confidently quiet.

I learned that not speaking much in social situations was actually quite good as long as I wasn't awkward about it. I only spoke when I had something interesting to add. I had this air of mystery about me that served me well at the time as I learned to listen, which helped me to grow my confidence and helped me pick up on the social cues of other people.

Again, this had a compounding effect on most other areas in my life and being confidently quiet quickly strengthened other empowering beliefs I needed to have in order to move forward in life.

I developed a "can-do" attitude, which increased that circular compound effect on my life overall. So, the belief of "I am confident socially," the starter belief, had a circular compounding effect, which came back round to strengthen my starter belief even more.

CHAPTER SUMMARY

———

- The story of how flipping the beliefs about potatoes fed a nation.

- The circular compound effect states that changing a starter belief will have an effect on a lot of other beliefs and comes back round to strengthen the original starter belief.

- The story of social confidence beliefs.

The Belief Principle

CHAPTER 7

Why Change Our Beliefs?

"It is not about the money you make; it is about the impact you make."

RUSSELL BRUNSON

That's a very good question you have to ask yourself: why change your beliefs?

If we break beliefs down to their simplest state, you have two different types of beliefs:

Disempowering or limiting beliefs. These beliefs hold us back from truly living a life of fullness and wellness and can even cause us physical and mental harm if we don't recognize them and acknowledge them.

Beliefs like: "I am not good enough," "I am not intelligent enough," "I am no good at (insert subject here)," "I am too old," or "I'll never have any money." All these beliefs and more hold us back. They stop us from growing as human beings, and our purpose in life is to grow as much as we can and to reach what Abraham Maslow calls Self Actualization.

Empowering beliefs. These beliefs drive us forward and help us to grow. These are the ones we should nurture and aim to install in our minds in order to help us reach our goals and our true potential in life. Nobody would have any goals in life if they didn't have some empowering beliefs, so you see, you have some empowering beliefs already.

To answer the question of why we need to change our beliefs to start our journey of self-discovery, it's to help us grow to reach our full potential.

Your beliefs just now reside within your comfort zone.

The beliefs you have about yourself reside within an area in your mind called your comfort zone. This is the place where nothing really challenges you and you are coasting along, minding your own business, and just getting on with life. And that's okay if you are happy with that, but a lot of us aren't happy—we want something more, something to challenge our mind, heart, and body. Life begins at the edge of your comfort zone.

The thing is, we cannot grow if we are not challenged in life. That's the reason we go to school to challenge our minds; that's the reason we go to the gym to challenge our bodies; that's the reason we start a business, write a book, network, speak in public, or take a new job—it's all to challenge ourselves.

Sometimes it can be tough, but the challenging journey we take when we go outside our comfort zone is so much better than the stagnation of staying inside it.

By challenging every area of your life, you will change your beliefs about yourself, about what you believe is possible, and your reality will change, sometimes overnight and sometimes over time.

CHAPTER SUMMARY

———

- We change our beliefs to get rid of limiting beliefs and to install new empowering beliefs that will drive us toward our goals in life.

- Your current beliefs reside within your comfort zone.

- Nobody grows outside their comfort zone.

- Challenge all areas of your life in order to grow in every way.

CHAPTER 8

It's All About Changing Your Identity

"The ultimate form of intrinsic motivation is when a habit becomes part of your identity. It's one thing to say I'm the type of person who wants this. It's something very different to say I'm the type of person who is this."

JAMES CLEAR

We've spoken about beliefs a lot (obviously, the book is about beliefs); however, deep down we are not just looking to change our beliefs. What we are looking to do is to change our identity.

When I first had the revelation that it wasn't just about the beliefs we have, it was about our identity, it took me even deeper down the rabbit hole of the mind and forced me to ask bigger questions about myself. It forced me to look at my life and ask:

Am I living life like the person I wish to become?

That question was huge for me, and hopefully, you get just how massive the question is.

After my initial research phase for this book, I sat down at my computer and started writing. I would sit for a few hours here and there and write away. However, it was not until I really took it seriously that things started to come alive in the book. I first had to identify as a writer before I took things to the next level.

One of the things I would do that made a big difference was, when asked "What do you do?" I would answer, "I am a writer and online trainer."

The previous answer to that question had been, "I have a business online, teaching various topics like social media, personal development and cryptocurrency."

So I had multiple identities, which is okay—we all do—but when it came to my business, I wanted to be known for personal development and specifically being a writer. My five-year plan was to write books around beliefs, become the go-to expert on that topic, and speak at events and conferences about it.

So I was now identifying myself as a writer.

When you identify with being something, you start to take on the beliefs, habits, values, and actions of that identity. So I took on the identity of a writer and wrote every day; I started the marketing before I even finished the book; I planted seeds to grow a reputation as the go-to expert on personal and business beliefs; I mixed with other authors online; I read as a writer instead of a reader. So I now have the identity of being a writer and then making the beliefs that come with being a writer a part of who I am.

Once I finish this book and get it published, that will strengthen my belief even more, and I will identify further with being a writer and strengthen everything about that identity for myself.

Not only will my belief about being a writer

become a trunk belief, it will also have branch and leaf beliefs that come from that trunk belief.

Your Multifaceted Identities

Being a writer is only part of who I am as a person. It's part of the multifaceted identities I have in life. You, too, have multifaceted identities in your life, and it's important to be in control of them by consciously asking yourself what identities you wish to have.

I am a husband, and I take that identity seriously by identifying what a good husband is and, I hope, living my life as a good husband. I am also a father, and I take that identity seriously, as well. We have to take the identities we have and be aware of them.

If you work for a company or organization and you don't like what you do, then you have to identify what you would like to do. Once you have done that, it will be much easier to change your identity. If you constantly complain about your job without actually trying to figure out what you want to do, then you're always going to be stuck.

It's the same if you are in a relationship that you don't like, whether romantically, work-based, friend-based or family-based.

The beliefs you have around your relationships will determine the boundaries you set. When those boundaries are broken, then your relationships are broken, and you'll know it's time to do something about it.

When you really think about it, it's the same for every single area of your life from your spiritual identity to your wealth identity; it all comes down to your beliefs about the different identities you have.

The Identity Shift Process

Every identity you wish to take on in your life comes with a set of beliefs that you must have. Some of the beliefs you will already possess, and some beliefs you will need to install. Some of the new beliefs will be very apparent from the outset, and some you will find along the way.

The process for an identity shift is as follows:

- Become aware of all the major beliefs you would need to have for the new identity.
- Pick out the new beliefs you need to install and start finding evidence for them.
- Continue to find and build on the evidence of each new belief until it becomes a part of your belief system.

So the first step in the identity shift process is to look at the beliefs of the identity you wish to have.

For me, to become an author, I had to think about the following beliefs:

- I have self-discipline I can write a book.
- I have something useful to share with the world I am confident.
- It's all about the readers I can build a following.
- I have the motivation.
- I have the tenacity to finish the book.
- The book is good enough to publish.

Those are just some of the main beliefs I need to have as an author. Some I already possess, e.g., I have something useful to share with the world, I can write a book, and a few others.

What I may not believe I have is the self-discipline to write a book, so I need to install that belief.

The second part of the process is to find evidence for the new beliefs you need to install. So using the example above with regards to the self-discipline belief, I need to first ask myself when I have shown self-discipline in my past:

- I have the self-discipline to have managed a blog for thirteen years.
- I have the self-discipline to have written more than one million words in more than 500 blog posts.
- I have the self-discipline to have done a live show every weekday for more than two years.
- I have the self-discipline to research every day in other parts of my business.
- I have had the self-discipline to sit down and write fiction books in the past.

So when I think about the belief of self-discipline, I actually find a lot of evidence to prove that I do have self-discipline and that I just need to sit down and start writing the book.

What I now need to work on is the belief that the book is good enough to publish. At first, I thought only external forces would be able to tell me if it's good enough to publish. Now, I know that my locus of control is internal. I need to find a publisher who believes the book is good enough if I publish the traditional route, or I can self-publish, as traditional publishing may take too long.

The third part is to continue to build up the evidence to prove that your new belief is true. This is extremely important, so any new actions that you take that confirm your new belief must be mentally noted. For example, over the last ten days I have sat down at the computer and completed one hour of research and writing per day, writing at least 500 words per day. This further strengthens my belief that I am self-disciplined.

The Key To Every Successful Person In The World

The key to success in any area of life is to have the beliefs of a successful person. When you have the beliefs, you then have the thoughts, actions, values, and habits of a successful person, and that is the key—it all starts with your beliefs.

This is why it is so important to look at the type of person you wish to become and then reverse engineer all the beliefs you need in order to become that person.

After you work on the beliefs, your thoughts, actions, values, and habits will naturally follow to help you assume the identity of the person you wish to be.

A Story Of Identity And Belief

In the early 1970's, Sylvester Stallone was a struggling actor trying to make his way in New York. He had a little success in a film called, *The Lords of Flatbush*.

Despite that success, Stallone admits, he was still so broke he had to go out and sell his dog, Butkis.

After feeling down and at one of his lowest points in his life, Stallone took himself to watch the Muhammad Ali vs. Chuck Wepner fight.

When Chuck Wepner knocked down Ali, Stallone was inspired and took it as a metaphor for life.

That metaphor for life gave Stallone an idea, and it was an idea that was going to change his life forever. In three days, he had most of the script written for a new movie. It was around ninety pages in length and was not finished yet. Only about a third of the original script was kept in the movie.

Later on, while on a casting call for another movie, he met Bob Chartoff and Irwin Winkler. It was clear that Stallone was not right for the part they were casting for. On the way out, Stallone told the two producers of the script he had written. They advised Stallone to bring the script around later on so they could read it.

"Originally, when I brought the script to them, they were fairly enthusiastic about it. The one thing they weren't enthusiastic about was me playing the part, and I really can't blame them. At the time Ryan O'Neal was a candidate, Burt Reynolds, Robert Redford, Jimmy Caan, and they were all at the top of their game."

They offered Stallone $360,000 for the script, with the condition that he wouldn't play Rocky. His $40 car had just blown up, he was taking the bus to work, he had $106 in the bank, and had to sell his dog to pay the bills.

Stallone knew he was the man for the main character in *Rocky* and turned down offer after offer.

That is real belief. Stallone knew what identity he wanted to have and would not be tempted from that identity because he had the belief and tenacity to stick to his beliefs.

The producers eventually relented and gave Stallone one million dollars to make the movie, starring himself. They came in under budget by using family and friends in the cast, shooting with handheld cameras, and only using one take to film most of the footage. One million dollars was an extremely low budget for a film, even in the 1970's.

When the movie started getting screened around Hollywood, it was well-received. But the real test was when it was screened at the Director's Guild in front of 900 industry types.

The theatre was packed, but the movie was playing terribly. Stallone told Michael Watson,

> "The laughs weren't coming where they were supposed to. The fight scenes seemed to be listless, as the response was. And I just sat there, as everyone left the theatre, and I couldn't believe it. I really blew it. I was humiliated and saddened by it. So I walked down three flights of stairs out of the theatre and everyone from the theatre was standing there waiting for me. And they started to applaud. I mean truly applaud. I'll never experience a moment like that again."

Rocky went on to receive nine Oscar nominations and three wins, including Best Picture, and grossed over $200 million.

Now, a lot of people would say it was reckless to turn down $360,000 when Stallone and his wife were poor and living on the breadline.

However, Stallone had a deep inner belief, and he had assumed the identity of someone who was successful. That is true grit, determination, and belief.

For me, it is one of the most inspirational stories ever. You can see the interview with Michael Watson on the resources page of this book at *www.thebeliefprinciple.com/resources*.

CHAPTER SUMMARY

———

- When you want to change a belief you are really changing a part of your identity.

- You have a multifaceted identity, so we change our beliefs according to the different identities we have.

- Each identity you have will come with a different set of beliefs, however, these beliefs can cross over into other identities.

- The key to every successful person in the world is adopting the beliefs of a successful person.

- The story of Sylvester Stallone and his undying belief in himself.

CHAPTER 9

The Big I Am

"Whatever follows the 'I am' will eventually find you."

JOEL OSTEEN

We've seen how a lot of our beliefs have been passed down to us as borrowed beliefs, but what about the beliefs we develop in our teenage and adult years?

I want to talk about an important part of our psychology, which I've termed, The Big I AM.

When I first grasped the significance of this, it was a huge revelation and a turning point in my life.

Hating My Job

Years ago, working as a homeless worker, I

really started to resent having to go to work each day. I knew that there was something else I was meant to be doing in life, mainly helping others through personal development writing. I loved helping others get back on their feet with the knowledge and training I had, but I identified my job as something that was rigid and an obstacle in my way of getting to where I wanted to go.

When asked, "What is it that you do?" I would say, "I am a homeless worker," always with an air of resentment.

That changed when I started to look at the job from another perspective.

I was getting paid to learn about the psychology of others. I was actually learning how people "tick" in a crisis. A lot of the service users I dealt with were abusing alcohol and drugs, and I was learning first-hand how the mind worked when under the influence of those substances and just how different that was to the general population.

In actual fact, what I realized was that we all act in similar ways when trying to deal with life.

When I started to see the job as a fluid, non-rigid endeavor, my perception changed and so did my disdain for the job.

As you know, I went on to help alcohol and drug abusers overcome their addictions—if that was their desire. I then started to see my job as a way to speed up the learning process while helping service users at the same time, and I was learning every day. My job was fluid. It served a purpose, both for the service users and for me. It was no longer a rigid obstacle to resent.

I believe that's where a lot of us are at the moment with our jobs.

Nominalization

There is a term in Neuro Linguistic Programming (NLP) called nominalization, which refers to verbs that have been turned into abstract nouns. This was hard to grasp for me at first, so here's how I thought about this example.

"There is no communication in our marriage"—the verb "communicate" has been turned into something static and rigid: communication.

This means that the communication in the marriage has nowhere to go. That's the way it is, and it can't be changed. When we say something like this, our minds automatically think, "Okay, there is no communication," and they will stop looking for solutions. It is a statement of fact, and as we know, facts are rigid. So, too, does the word communicate become rigid in this example.

Instead we could say, "How can we communicate better in our marriage?"

By asking this question, your mind automatically starts looking for solutions. It does this in so many different ways, and it can bring up answers when we least suspect they will appear in a bookshop, in the bath, while reading a book or driving home from work.

Your subconscious mind is busy marinating the question and thinking about solutions while you get on with day-to-day living. Sometimes it will throw up answers just to let you know it is still working on the problem, and that is the beauty of the mind.

A lot of us have nominalized ourselves in a lot of aspects of our lives. One of the biggest culprits that we use in language is the phrase "I am."

For example:

- "I am no good at math."
- "I am an alcoholic."
- "I am no good with money."
- "I am a terrible sleeper."
- "I am an idiot."
- "I am poor."

All the phrases above, when spoken, leave the mind nowhere to go. So the mind just says, "Okay, I am no good with money, no point in trying to be better, as that's the way 'I AM.'"

It is a rigid statement of fact, and a fact has nowhere to go.

Imagine being told as a child that you are no good at math. You develop a deep belief in that "fact," and as soon as you look at algebra, your mind has already shut down to the idea of you being able to do anything with algebra as you are no good at math because you've been told and told yourself hundreds of times that it's true.

De-Nominalizing Your Life

What we want to do is feed the mind and let it help us find solutions and become fluid again instead of rigid. So when we ask our mind a question, it gets to work in the background looking for solutions, instead of stating a fact.

In my old job, a lot of people defined themselves as alcoholics. They would say that's just who they were. What I tried to do was to let them see that their drinking patterns had gotten out of control and teach them new ways of thinking to better control their drinking, therefore de-nominalizing their identification with being an alcoholic.

When someone says, "I am an alcoholic," it is a statement of fact and has nowhere to go, and that person will always identify with the behavior and actions of an alcoholic.

I know AA is not going to like this, but I do not agree with someone standing up at an AA meeting and saying, "My name is…and I am an alcoholic" even after ten years of not drinking alcohol.

Don't get me wrong—the first step to overcoming alcohol issues is to admit them to yourself and others, and I understand someone standing up and saying this at a meeting in order for them to truly admit it, but after six months, I believe the term should be dropped.

Instead, I would rather someone stand up and say, "My name is...and I have not drunk alcohol for six months."

The Language Of A Belief

Sometimes the way we speak to ourselves is disgraceful. We would never speak to a friend the way we often speak to ourselves. This is why it is so important to think about the way you speak to yourself, as it can have a dramatic impact on your life.

Think about when you've done something wrong: even if no one was around to witness it, you berate yourself and belittle yourself for a silly mistake. I have often put myself down for taking a wrong turn when driving somewhere; what's that all about?!

Berating yourself like this is usually a natural reaction to your past when you've been berated by someone else for making a mistake. Well, it's time to stop doing that to yourself. You no longer have to please or impress anybody when you're alone. Now if I were to take a wrong turn on a journey, I don't even think about the mistake.

I just turn around and get back on the right road.

Just as we berate ourselves when making a mistake, we often use language that will stop the formation of an empowering belief. I don't just mean I AM statements.

Take a look at **TABLE 1. The Language Of Beliefs** on the next page and find out how you can change the way you talk to yourself to help strengthen your beliefs in every area of your life.

Can you see other areas of your life where you are using language like this that is installing beliefs instead of installing empowering beliefs?

TABLE 1. The Language Of Beliefs	
OLD WAY	**NEW WAY**
I am no good with computers	I am learning all about computers
I could never do that	I could do that
I am an idiot	I am learning all the time
I am poor	I am getting better with money
I am such a loser	I will win this battle
I can't do that	I will do this
I am always sick	I am feeling healthier all the time
I am not intelligent enough	I am going to learn this
I am fat	I am getting healthier
I am an alcoholic	I no longer drink alcohol
I am not attractive	I am f***ing gorgeous
I hope I'll make it	I will make it somehow
I am okay	I am great
I will be happy when…	I am very happy
I don't know	I will find that out
She is so lucky	She deserves that

CHAPTER SUMMARY

———

- The Big I AM determines and affirms the different beliefs you have about yourself.

- Nominalization are verbs that have been turned into abstract nouns and we need to look at this in terms of how we talk to ourselves.

- De-nominalizing your life involves speaking to yourself in such a way as to find solutions and not be rigid about a particular problem.

- The language of your beliefs will determine how successful you are in a particular area of your life.

CHAPTER 10

Your Belief Filter

"Imagination is the only weapon in the war against reality."

LEWIS CARROLL

Have you ever taken a picture with your phone and then been given an array of filters to touch the photo up with? These tools can be useful, but on Snapchat alone, there are over 300,000 custom lenses now available. The world has gone selfie and filter crazy.

Well, the world you live in is being seen through the eyes of your filters, and your filters are your beliefs. Since you have hundreds of different beliefs about yourself and the world around you, you then have the potential to see the world totally anew every day, particularly when you mix feelings into the equation, but we won't talk about that just now.

For now, imagine for a few minutes that you have won the lottery. You've got five million pounds in your account. You are beside yourself with excitement. You think about everything you're going to do with the money, the experiences you're going to have, the countries you will visit, the lovely house you can buy, and all the people you can help with the money. How does that feel? What kind of thoughts run through your mind?

You no longer have any money worries, you can pack in that job you've never liked, and you can buy a new car. When you picture this and feel this scene, imagine looking out of the window of your home—what does it look like outside?

Seriously—describe what it looks like for a few seconds.

Many of you will have said the sun is shining, it's colorful, you probably imagined it in summertime, you can see your new car, your kids are happy, your partner is happy, and you're all jolly and spiffingly delirious with happiness.

Even imagining this scene in your mind changes your internal energy, and you can't help but feel a little excited.

Can you imagine what that would actually do to your beliefs in your life? You would feel more confident, you would have no debts, which would help you throw out all your limiting money worries (at least for a short period), you could finally travel, you would no longer have to dream about that house you've always wanted, or you could buy that house by the sea and just spend your days reading and writing books (what a life that would be). So you see how old beliefs would immediately be eliminated and new beliefs would immediately be installed?

Okay, back to real life now.

That quick exercise was to show you that the world you live in is seen through the eyes of your belief filters. If you manage to change your beliefs, you can change the way you see the world, and if you change the way you see the world, you can have a much better quality of life, be more action oriented, have more energy, and attract more of the things and people you want in life.

Now think about a time when you were really sad and a time when you were really happy. The world does not look or feel the same in these opposing ends of the same spectrum.

Happiness and sadness are all part of one spectrum, and at any given moment, you are either veering towards happiness or veering towards sadness to varying degrees.

People who are depressed for a prolonged period of time have found it difficult to climb their way back to the other end of the spectrum and feel happier.

Depression is not an absence of happiness—it's the feeling that happiness may never return. We are talking about persistent depressive disorder here and not the many other types.

If you've ever had a depressive episode, you know that the world looks totally different than when you've been extremely happy for a period of time. This is, in part, due to temporary belief shifts, possibly lots of them.

So what does this tell us?

It tells us that our beliefs are fluid and can be heavily influenced by the way we feel.

The Feelings Of Beliefs

Why do we not visit the doctor when we are feeling extremely happy for prolonged periods of time?

You might be thinking, "What?! What is he going on about, going to the doctors due to feeling happy!"

It does seem absurd. But when we are feeling down for a prolonged period of time, we go to the doctor, who then reinforces our initial thoughts that we are suffering from depression.

Remember the I AM statements—"I AM suffering from depression" or "I have depression."

We are given pills to help us overcome that depression by way of pharmaceuticals, which stimulate parts of our brain to release the happy hormones, mainly dopamine, endorphins, oxytocin, and serotonin.

The Spotlight Effect

When we ask the question, "Why do some people feel happy all the time?" we will quickly find a way to help people with mild depression.

The answer to the question is it's because happy people focus on feeling great. Our emotions flow where our focus goes.

So if we constantly focus on the light in the world, then we can't keep our attention on the darkness. Think of your thoughts at any given point as a bright spotlight. When you shine that spotlight on positive thoughts, the negative thoughts are left in the dark.

It's only when we put a spotlight on the "depressing" thoughts that the periods of depression come to us. If we focus on these "depressing" thoughts for a prolonged period of time, we begin to get used to them always being in the spotlight.

So we have to shift our focus. Can it really be that easy? Yes, it can. In a systematic review of literature on the topic of positive psychology for the treatment of depression, it was found that treating people who had depression to varying degrees with positive psychology was useful:

"Increasing positive emotion, developing personal forces, seeking direction, meaning and engagement for the daily patient proved to be important and meaningful strategies for reducing the signs and symptoms and relapse, to applicants in depression." (*Clin. Pract. Epidemiol. Ment. Health.* 2013; 9: 221–237. "The Role of Positive Emotion and Contributions of Positive Psychology in Depression Treatment: Systematic Review.")

Here's one amazing tip that could change your life: Stop watching, listening to, or reading the news.

In a question on *Quora*, someone asked:

I'm a news junkie, but it's making me depressed. How do I break my addiction to watching/reading news?

Here was my reply to this person:

Watching the news constantly is one of the worst things you can do, in my opinion.

The news is disproportionately biased towards bad news—why? Because unfortunately, bad news sells. And it's not only a little disproportionate, it's biased in the extreme.

If I listened to and read the news every day, I would feel so depressed thinking that the world is a terrible place full of fear, hate-filled people, rapists, pedophiles, murderers, and muggers, but it's not. The news gathers all the worst stories and condenses them into one newspaper or show, but it doesn't report on the millions of people who are good, who help others, who are changing the world in a positive way.

That's because for every terrible news story, there are a million (total guesstimate) good stories out there.

Not only that, but all the newspapers, news channels, and news shows have their own agendas and really ramp up on the propaganda.

So think about this: most of us believe what we see and hear in the news because it has to be true if CNN or the BBC are reporting it.

Your Belief Filter

We are not choosing the news stories, they are being fed to us, BUT the news stories are fed to the big news channels by the government, corporations, and anyone in a position of power. Then that news is filtered down to the smaller news channels, which means it is being shown EVERYWHERE.

Ask yourself this question: Will it make ANY difference in YOUR life knowing that the likes of Oscar Pistorius killed his girlfriend or not? No, not one little bit of difference, and it's the same with most news stories out there; they don't make one little bit of difference to our lives at all.

Does it help knowing politicians are corrupt? Does it help knowing that there are "Severed heads found in a Mexico Grave"? Does it help knowing that "Trump Makes Thanksgiving Unity Call"?

Instead, YOU CHOOSE what your mind is fed by watching positive TV shows and films and reading books that will lift you up instead of making you feel the world is a shit place. YouTube has some brilliant channels to make you feel better about life, there are millions of books out there that make you feel good, and there are great TV shows that uplift you, as well.

It's not to say you ignore the bad shit that happens in the world—you know it goes on, but you don't need to be reminded of it every single day. You might say that you need to know what's going on in the world — I'm here to tell you that YOU DON'T.

One good rule: ask yourself, "Will this make any difference whatsoever in my life or my family's life?" About 99.99 percent of the time, it won't.

Be the leader of your own mind and decide what information goes in and out. Take the step to have a news fast for thirty days and see what difference it makes in your life— guaranteed it will be life-changing. (*Quora.com*, www.quora.com/Im-a-news-junkie-but-its-making-me-depressed-How-do-I-break-my-addiction-to-watching-reading-news).

Think about what you've been focusing your thoughts on today. Chances are that what you've been thinking about has a direct correlation to how you feel.

If you have these feelings and thoughts for long enough, they will pretty soon start to mold themselves into a belief, and that belief will become a filter through which you view and judge the world, so be careful what you think about.

Changing You Filters

You have around 60,000 thoughts per day (goodness knows who came up with that number) and 95-98 percent of those thoughts are the same one's day in and day out—or rather, the same types of thoughts. Let's do some math here:

95% of 60,000 = 57,000

That means 57,000 thoughts that were the same as—or the same type as—yesterday. We can guesstimate that about 10,000 of those thoughts are about getting up in the morning, planning our day ahead, driving to school or work, practical thinking about issues at work or home, etc.—these are practical thoughts that we have to think about day in and day out.

So we are left with around 47,000 thoughts.

That's 47,000 spare thoughts that are up for grabs and could be turned into something useful. What do you think these thoughts are about? Here are some classifications of the 47,000 thoughts we have:

Worry, boredom, daydreaming, future planning, catastrophizing, fighting in our minds, negative self-talk, positive self-talk, what others think of us, and so on.

With how many of those 47,000 spare thoughts each day do we think positively about the future, or plan positively for the future, or ask the right questions to get a better future? I am willing to guess not very many at all.

Our minds are in a constant battle with useless worry (not all worry is bad if you do something useful with it), other people inside our heads, self-pity, self-deprecation, negative thinking, despair, doom, and gloom.

Changing the lens through which you see the world could start with what you focus on every day. If you make a conscious effort to focus on the more positive things in life, I guarantee your mood will shift.

If you do this long enough, your beliefs start to shift and veer towards the positive.

The more evidence you gather about the world being an amazing place to live in, the stronger your positive beliefs will become.

After that, your actions begin to change, and you will find you're a little happier and more confident. Then your habits begin to change, then your values change, and pretty soon your life has changed.

These imperceptible little changes will make a huge difference in your life. When you do this, you will start to notice little things that perpetuate your beliefs that the world is a good place and good things do happen for you. That's all to do with the energy we spoke about earlier and the fact that you will attract more of what you think.

CHAPTER SUMMARY

- Your belief filter means that you see the world through the filter of all your different personal beliefs. Therefore, everyone's reality and world are completely different.

- The feelings of your beliefs are just as important as the beliefs you are trying to install or get rid of.

- The spotlight effect means that what we focus on will grow, whether it's good or bad.

- Changing your filters means changing the thoughts you have every day.

CHAPTER 11

Your Belief Ceiling

"You cannot grow beyond the level of your beliefs."

STEVEN AITCHISON

The belief ceiling is something we've all come across, yet we may not have realized it.

Think about your job now or maybe a previous job you held. When you first joined the company, hopefully you liked the job and thought of ways to climb through the ranks.

Then something happened at an unconscious level: you hit a ceiling, a belief ceiling that stopped you from going all the way to the top.

You maybe brushed it off and made excuses for it, saying things like, "I've not got the right face," "I didn't really want it," or "I wouldn't be able to cope with the stress," yet despite the excuses, you were disappointed. Well, I have to tell you the only thing that stopped you was the belief ceiling whereby you had a set belief of how far you could go in the company, and your belief ceiling was always going to stop you from going further.

I told you the story of how I grew my company into a six-figure business but had to do it at different stages of the belief ceiling. I told you that during my first year in business, my belief was that I could earn $30,000 in sales, and I earned very close to $30,000 in that year. I then told myself I could earn $60,000 in the next year of business, and again I hit $60,000 that year.

The next year, I doubled my expectations and doubled my belief to $130,000, the next year $250,000 and the year after that to $500,000, but I didn't quite reach it (I actually managed $330,000 in sales income that year).

Then I switched direction in my business, and my new expectation for sales in my first year in a completely new field of cryptocurrency was around $100,000. Guess what?

Your Belief Ceiling

In 2019, I brought in $100,000 in sales from my cryptocurrency program and my other income streams, and 60 percent of it came from cryptocurrency sales.

There's a strange thing that happens when you've had success like I did from 2015 to 2017: your belief ceiling is automatically raised in everything that you do. So I was starting in a brand-new niche, but my expectation was much higher than before, as my beliefs about my own abilities had changed so much over the years.

This is the same phenomenon we see when some business owners go completely bankrupt and have to start from scratch. You will often find that they come back bigger and stronger than ever before due to their internal belief systems changing so dramatically.

This is what will happen to you if you work at this. I'm not suggesting you start a business (unless that is your goal!); I am talking about everyday life. Pretty soon you will come to a point where you believe in yourself so much that you will try anything you want to simply because you believe you can do it.

And the good thing is even if you try something new and don't succeed the first time, you will have built up enough resilience to push yourself to keep trying.

That is the perfect example of the belief ceiling in action, and it's something we unconsciously use all the time. It's time to get rid of the belief ceilings in your life.

This happens with large companies, too. Often when they change their internal mission statements or a set of beliefs by which they want to run their company, their success can turn around dramatically. Here's a list of a few companies that have or have nearly gone bankrupt, only to come back much stronger:

Apple. It is hard to believe that the world's largest company by market capitalization was once in dire straits. While never actually filing for bankruptcy, Apple (AAPL) was on the verge of going bust in 1997. At the last minute, arch-rival Microsoft (MSFT) swooped in with a $150 million investment and saved the company. People have speculated that Microsoft only did so because it was worried that regulators would regard it as a monopoly without the competition from Apple in the marketplace.

General Motors. Following the financial crisis of 2008 and the Great Recession, General Motors (GM), once the largest automobile manufacturer in the world, filed for bankruptcy and was ultimately bailed out by the U.S. federal government. In December 2013, the U.S. Department of the Treasury fully exited its investment in GM, recovering a total of $39.7 billion from its original investment of $51 billion.

Ally Bank. Ally bank, now Ally Financial (ALLY), was the auto-financing arm of General Motors, extending credit to purchasers of its cars. The bank was bailed out alongside its parent to the tune of $17 billion by the U.S. Department of the Treasury. The company emerged as a profitable business with a market capitalization of $11 billion and just reported better-than-expected earnings — double analysts' expectations.

Chrysler. General Motors wasn't the only car maker to go bust in 2008. American car manufacturer Chrysler (FCAU) was actually the first to fall. Despite a $4 billion government bailout package, the company was forced to declare bankruptcy in 2009. It was later purchased by European car maker Fiat and has seen above average success and growth since.

Marvel Entertainment. With blockbuster movies such as *Spiderman*, *The Avengers*, and *Guardians of the Galaxy*, it is surprising to note that the company filed for bankruptcy in 1996. This was before the company got into the movie-making business, when it focused solely on comic books.

Today, the company's properties are worth billions of dollars with millions of fans around the world.

Six Flags. Theme park operator and amusement company Six Flags (SIX) has eighteen regional theme and water parks throughout North America, home to some of the world's biggest and fastest roller coasters. In 2009, however, the company declared bankruptcy after racking up more than $2.5 billion in debt which it could not pay back.

Texaco. Now a thriving part of Chevron (CVX), Texaco was once one of the most dominant integrated oil companies in the world. A legal dispute with competitor Pennzoil in the 1980s, however, caused it to file bankruptcy: Pennzoil asserted that Texaco owed it $10.5 billion, which Texaco couldn't pay.

Sbarro. Operating and franchising more than 1,100 fast food style pizza and Italian food restaurants worldwide, they went bankrupt twice: first through a Chapter 11 bankruptcy reorganization in 2011 and then again in 2014. The company has re-emerged with the help of a collaboration of private equity firms to transform the company's image to a faster casual style, rather than its previous kiosk or food counter concept.

(List courtesy of *Investopedia.com*, 2015: www.investopedia.com/articles/personal-finance/051115/7-bankrupt-companies-came-back.asp).

CHAPTER SUMMARY

———

- Your belief ceiling will determine exactly how far you can go in life with a particular belief.

- Personal story of my own belief ceiling and how I changed it to become wealthier.

- Sharing the stories of companies that have hit rock bottom and come back again.

CHAPTER 12

The Energy Of Beliefs

"Everything is energy and energy is everything."

MARIA FLYNN

In this chapter, I would like to start with a simple exercise to show you just how powerful your mind is.

First of all, I'd like you to record your resting heart rate.

To do this, hold out your right hand and turn it palm facing upwards.

Next, take your forefinger and middle finger of your left hand and gently place them on the top of your wrist on the outside edge.

You'll feel a pulsing, which is your heartbeat.

The Belief Principle

Count how many beats there are in a fifteen-second period, then multiply the figure by four to get your resting BPM (beats per minute).

Don't worry, this will all become clear, and if you've never taken your own heart rate before, then you've learned something new today— every day is a school day.

Once you have done this and you have written your resting BPM down, I'd like you to sit and think about the following scenario in your mind:

It's a warm summer's day, and you are jogging up a steep hill into a forest area. You are getting slightly breathless as the climb is getting steeper with every step you take. The sweat drips from your forehead into your eyes. Your legs are aching, but you keep running. The sun beats down harder on you.

You keep running and speed up, you can feel your heart pumping... bang... bang... bang... you're getting hotter, you're breathless, you're panting, but still you run faster.

You see up ahead of you the road coming to an end, and you run ever faster, you're getting really breathless now, your heart seems to pound out of your chest, and your legs ache. You speed up even more...only this time you notice you're actually just about to run off the edge of a cliff...your toes at the very edge of the road and you see below how far you would have fallen, thousands of feet...

Now, immediately after picturing that scenario in your mind, record your heart rate as you did before: for fifteen seconds and then multiply it by four to get your BPM.

What happened?

If you really pictured that scenario in your mind's eye, the chances are that your heart rate increased quite significantly.

What you have just done is controlled your heart rate with the power of your mind. There was nothing else involved in this; no real exercise, no running, and no nearly falling off the edge of a cliff. It was ALL in your mind, and yet you were able to increase your heart rate.

That is the power you have, that is the power your mind has, and that is the power YOU have to control your mind and body. Yet for all this power, we still have limiting beliefs that hold us back in life.

The scenario you just went through in your mind was you creating energy. Your thoughts were the trigger for the energy, and your mind and biological functions were the source of that energy.

We also get energy from outside sources, but that's for another chapter.

You can now see that a lot of stress comes from anxious thoughts. People who are stressed have the same recurring thoughts throughout the day, which leads to stress hormones being released from the brain such as cortisol, which leads to chronic stress, which in turn leads to a lot of other health problems.

So imagine then the energy your beliefs hold. If your thoughts have the power to trigger energetic reactions like the above inside your body, then think about the energy that is constantly used with your limiting beliefs—but that energy is being used and drained in the background and goes unnoticed.

Your Beliefs Are Your Apps

It's a little like your mobile phone. Your phone only holds so much charge when it is not connected to a power source. The charge may only last for around ten hours or so, but if you have too many apps open in the background, the charge will run down a lot quicker.

Your beliefs are the apps that are running in the background. You'll quickly feel drained if you don't get control of your limiting beliefs.

Think about it this way: if you have twenty apps running in the background on your mobile phone, the energy would be drained within an hour or so. If you have multiple limiting beliefs running in the background, your mental energy will be constantly drained.

This constant draining leaves little room for you to accept the creative and vibrant energy you need to get you through life to feel happy, confident, successful, and joyful.

Going back to the mobile phone analogy again, not all apps drain the same amount of energy from your battery.

There are apps that will drain a lot of energy and apps that will drain very little. For example, Snapchat, WhatsApp, and Netflix are among the apps that will drain your phone battery the fastest. So it would be wise to always shut those apps down when you finish using them.

The same goes for your limiting beliefs. There are big, hairy, audacious limiting beliefs that really drain you, and small, less hairy limiting beliefs that won't affect you much.

For now, the core limiting beliefs—which we labelled earlier as root beliefs—are the beliefs we want to focus on, as these are the ones that drain the most energy from your body, mind, and soul.

I want to leave you with a thought exercise.

Imagine if you believed you could literally do anything you put your mind too. If you wanted to learn speed reading, you have the confidence to do it; if you wanted to become an expert in computing, you have the confidence to do it; if you want to meet new people, if you want to live on your own, if you want to write a book, or if you want to do anything…you have the confidence to do it.

Imagine how that would feel. Think about this for a few minutes: what would you do if you knew you would be able to anything with relative ease?

Now I want you to think about the energy those thoughts created when you were thinking about what you'd love to do. That is the energy of your beliefs, and I want to help you create more energy like this.

The energy of your beliefs does not only affect your mind and body but touches others, as well, quite literally. Your energy is projected outwards, although it's an unseen force.

We have all come across people who can walk into a room full of strangers and totally stand out without saying a word.

That is their energy touching yours.

If our energy can touch others physically and yet not be seen, we have to ask, what is energy?

Everything In Life Is Vibration

Albert Einstein said that "everything in life is vibration," and he was right. Everything you see around you can be broken down to atoms. These atoms are in a constant state of motion, and depending on the vibration speed of these atoms, things appear as a solid, liquid, or gas. Sound is also a vibration, and so are thoughts.

Everything that manifests itself in your life is there because it matches the vibration from your thoughts. We're getting into another realm with that statement, but it's a seed I would like to plant in your mind to come back to later.

A table that appears solid is actually created by an underlying vibration.

Humans, too, are all big balls of atoms vibrating at different energy levels, and these atoms emit electrical energy. This energy can be felt by others in a subtle, invisible way.

Now, you don't need to believe this for it to be true; however, I'd like you to think back to a time in your life when everything just seemed to go right.

The Energy Of Beliefs

You met the right people, you got that job you were after, you made the money you needed, and you found the partner you'd always hoped for; everything was going just swimmingly. How does that happen, and how does it all happen at the same time?

It is due to your vibrational energy. When something good happens, you literally vibrate at a different energy frequency from before, those electrical signals in your body touch other people, and you are changing their energy into a higher vibrational energy which makes them feel good about themselves.

The people around you aren't thinking about atoms and vibrational energy—they only see that they feel good when you are around and naturally want to be around you more.

Now when that person feels good and their vibrational energy is lifted, they then spread that energy to the people close to them, who in turn do the same. So you literally start a wave of high vibrational energy with the people around you, and pretty soon that ONE good thing that happened to you has managed to touch the lives of thousands of people around you, and you don't even know it. Pretty cool, eh?

Okay, so because you have lifted your energy with one piece of good news and you are lifting the energy vibration of those around you, more good things will naturally come to you, and more opportunities will open up because people are very receptive to you, i.e., they are receiving your energy.

Due to all of this, people react differently towards you:

The job interviewers get a certain feeling about you and give you the job, your future partner was vibrating on the same frequency as you and was immediately attracted to you, your friends ask you if there's something different about you as you seem more "vibrant," you get that promotion, you get the loan you needed for your business, you have more energy to complete the book you always wanted to write, and you're feeling as if you're on fire.

We've all had these experiences in our lives, and the more this happens, the more we start to develop a belief that good things happen to us all the time.

This belief keeps us in a high state of vibrational energy, and we find it easier to lift ourselves out of a funk whenever we hit it.

However, this is not a belief that a lot of us have, and that's because we've not really been taught the energy of beliefs or the energy of our bodies or the energy of our thoughts.

Similarly, we've all had times when nothing seems to go right for us, and that is, again, due to the vibrational energy we are emitting.

Now that you know about this energy, can you see that your life is how it is just now, in part, due to the vibrational energy you have, whether it's high vibrational energy or low vibrational energy?

In his book, *You Are the Placebo: Making Your Mind Matter*, Joe Dispenza states:

"When you change your energy, you lift matter to a new mind, and your body vibrates at a faster frequency. You become more energy and less matter—more wave and less particle. The more elevated the emotion or the higher the creative state of mind, the more energy you have to rewrite the programs in the body. Your body then responds to a new mind."

So why are we sometimes stuck in the same vibrational energy all the time?

That is down to the beliefs you have. Your beliefs all have a vibrational energy, as well.

Try to get a picture of the person who holds these beliefs:

- Nobody should be trusted.
- Nothing good ever happens to me.
- I attract all the wrong people in life I am not good enough.
- I'll never be able to earn more money than I do now I never have any luck.
- I don't have anything to feel happy about.

What type of person did you imagine as you were reading the above beliefs? Certainly someone that could use help; however, these are not uncommon beliefs.

Millions of people around the world have installed them, unconsciously, into their bodies.

Can you see why this type of person will perpetuate their feelings of hopelessness?

Whenever they come into contact with someone, their vibrational energy is screaming "Stay away from me!" and so the cycle of hopelessness continues.

What can we do to change that?

We can change our root, trunk, branch, and even our leaf beliefs (more on that in a later chapter).

When we change our root and trunk beliefs, we literally change the energy with which we vibrate. Incidentally, if you've ever wondered why the law of attraction works, it has all to do with your vibrational energy, but it wasn't really explained well enough, and a lot of people brushed it off as pseudo-science. Now you have a working explanation as to why we attract what we believe.

You can change your whole vibrational energy by changing just one belief. In this book I am going to give you seven beliefs that WILL change your life in a short space of time.

These seven beliefs will ignite in you an unstoppable fire of higher vibrational energy that will help you get the things you want in life.

Sounds too good to be true, doesn't it?

Well, I am living proof.

I am sitting in a cafe in the West End of Glasgow called Offshore writing this book. When I moved to Glasgow in 1993, I used to visit the West End on nights out in Ashton Lane and Hillhead. The place has a completely different energy from anywhere else in Glasgow, and I always wanted to buy a flat here, but they were far out of my budget.

Every time I visited the Botanic Gardens to study while I was at the university, I kept telling myself, "I will be living here someday."

That was in 1997-2000.

In 2019, my wife and I bought a flat just off Byers Road in the heart of the West End. We totally love it and it's all down to the beliefs I installed over twenty years ago, and the beliefs my wife installed before I met her.

Don't worry—you don't have to wait twenty years for something to happen in your life. This book is designed to drastically reduce the time it takes to change your old beliefs and install new ones.

If I'd had this book twenty years ago, I am sure I would have been living in the West End years ago; however, everything happens as it should.

One thing you have to remember: wherever you are in your life right now is where you are meant to be in order to get to where you want to go.

Everything happens as it should, including you reading these words in whatever format that may be.

CHAPTER SUMMARY

———

- A simple exercise to show how powerful your mind is.

- All of your beliefs have the power to release and hold back energy.

- Your beliefs as apps. This is the analogy that all your beliefs are like apps on your phone…some good, some bad.

- Everything in life is energy and when we tap into that fact, we change the way we interact with the world.

CHAPTER 13

The Belief Placebo

"And can you teach your body emotionally what it would feel like to believe in this way…to be empowered…to be moved by your own greatness… to be invincible…to have courage… to be in love with life…to feel unlimited…to live as if your prayers are already answered?…"

JOE DISPENZA

There's a phenomenon in the medical world known as the placebo effect. I want to show you what this is and just how powerful it is. I would also like to show you how we can use the placebo effect to our benefit.

What Is The Placebo Effect?

A placebo is a medical treatment or procedure designed to deceive the participant in a clinical experiment setting. It does not contain any active ingredients but can often still produce a physical effect on the individual. For instance, sometimes the person's symptoms may improve. Or the person may have what appears to be side effects from the treatment. These responses are known as the "placebo effect."

There are some conditions in which a placebo can produce results even when people know they are taking a placebo. Studies show that placebos can have an effect on conditions such as:

- Depression
- Pain
- Sleep disorders
- Irritable bowel syndrome
- Menopause

In one study involving asthma, people using a placebo inhaler did no better on breathing tests than those sitting and doing nothing. But when researchers asked for people's perception of how they felt, the placebo inhaler was reported as being as effective as medicine in providing relief.

There are literally thousands of medical articles written about the power of placebos, and it has fascinated me to read these.

The fact that the mind can trick the body to elicit a physical response is amazing for us to know and something we can use to our advantage.

How Do Placebos Actually Work?

According to an article published on *medicalnewstoday.com* (www.medicalnewstoday.com/articles/306437.p h), there are four factors involved in the placebo effect:

1. Expectation and conditioning. Part of the power of the placebo lies in the expectations of the individual taking them. These expectations can relate to the treatment, the substance, or the prescribing doctor.

2. The placebo effect and the brain. Brain imaging studies have found measurable changes in the neural activity of people experiencing placebo analgesia. Areas that have been implicated include parts of the brain stem, spinal cord, nucleus accumbens, and amygdala.

3. Psychoneuroimmunology. This is a relatively new area of scientific study. It studies the direct effect of brain activity on the immune system. Just as a dog can be conditioned to salivate at the sound of a bell, so can mice be conditioned to restrain their immune system when presented with a specific stimulus.

4. Evolved health regulation. The body of a mammal has developed helpful physiological responses to pathogens.

For instance, fever is the result of an increase in our internal temperature to help kill bacteria and viruses. However, as these responses come at a cost, the brain decides when it will carry out a certain response.

So now that we know about the power of placebo and we know that it can still work even if we know it's a placebo, how do we use that to our advantage?

Creating Your Own Placebos

Imagine being able to create a pill with no side

effects, natural ingredients, no drowsiness and can ONLY create benefit for you.

You can if you wish, take a bottle of vitamin C tablets from the local health food store and turn them into powerful placebo pills whereby you tell the pill what you want it to do e.g. enhance my cognitive abilities.

We can create a contract with our body and our minds and tell our bodies that the vitamin C pill we are taking is a powerful cognitive enhancer which will help improve memory, makes us feel more alert, help us to stay focused longer, and help us retain information.

You might be laughing just now and saying this is ridiculous, how can you fool your body into believing that?

Look at the four factors above again and you'll see why this can work.

At first your mind will reject the notion that this vitamin C pill can have any affect whatsoever, but if you give it a chance and do it often enough your mind will come round to the idea that this pill is a powerful neuro cognitive enhancer.

I debated whether I should put the section on "creating your own placebos" in the book for ethical reasons, but I compromised and put a much-shortened version of the original text in here.

CHAPTER SUMMARY

- The placebo effect: A placebo is a medical treatment or procedure designed to deceive the participant in a clinical experiment setting. It does not contain any active ingredients but can often still produce a physical effect on the individual.

- How do placebos work?
  1. Expectation and conditioning.
  2. Placebo effect and the brain.
  3. Psychoneuroimmunology.
  4. Evolved health regulation.

- Creating your own placebos can be very powerful.

The Belief Principle

CHAPTER 14

The Rules Within Your Beliefs

*"Learn the rules like a pro, so you can
break them like an artist."*

PABLO PICASSO

Embedded in all of our root beliefs are the rules
by which we live our lives. They protect us from
feeling harmed and protect our emotional
homeostasis, so the rules are for self-
preservation. Root beliefs are very subjective
and cannot be tested easily or indeed proven to
anyone but ourselves. We can, however, test
the rules that have been created by our root
beliefs.

If you believe that you are not intelligent, your
rules might be as follows:

- Don't try too hard in school.
- Don't mix with intelligent people.

- Don't apply for university.
- Don't talk too much in front of people in case you sound stupid.
- Don't pursue intellectual hobbies.
- Don't ask someone out who you think is more intelligent than you.

If you were to break one of the rules above, it might lead to your belief "I am not intelligent" being strengthened. For example, if you said something in front of a group of people and they laughed at you for sounding stupid, it would strengthen your belief and hold you back in life.

When you live by the rules of the root belief "I am not intelligent," you subconsciously protect yourself from ever getting into the situation where this belief will be validated.

It's crazy, isn't it, that our minds would self-sabotage us like this, but our brains are only trying to protect us. Having said this, we cannot grow as human beings if we do not step outside our comfort zone.

Growth lies outside our comfort zone; stagnation and safety lie within it.

So we have to endure some emotional pain in order to grow, which is what we've been doing all of our lives at a subconscious level— the difference is we're making it work for us at a conscious level.

Let's look at another example and the rules associated with it.

If you believe that you don't deserve money in your life, some of the rules you live by might include:

- Never think about starting a business of your own.
- Don't invest your money, as you will lose it.
- Don't try new money-making opportunities.
- Being in debt is natural, and it's how everyone lives.
- There's no point in saving for the future.
- Only rich people get richer.
- I'll always be living from month to month.

Living by root belief rules means we cannot contradict a belief and therefore we do not try and change it. When we start to question a belief, remember, that's when it becomes malleable and open to change.

In the next section, I am going to show you how to uncover your beliefs and therefore your rules of life. You will be amazed at just how much you have held yourself back.

CHAPTER SUMMARY

———

- The rules within your beliefs will help, or hinder, you when it comes to moving forward in life.

- Knowing these rules can be extremely useful to know when trying to get rid of a limiting belief or install a new belief.

The Belief Principle

CHAPTER 15

Affirmations

*"You have unconsciously been using affirmations
every day of your life, which has helped
shape your beliefs."*

STEVEN AITCHISON

Actor and comedian James Eugene Carrey was
born on January 17, 1962, in Newmarket,
Ontario, Canada. Carrey got his start with a
spot doing stand-up at a Toronto comedy club
when he was just 15 years old.

By 1979, he had left the factory job as a janitor
he had taken in 1978 to help support his family
and was making his living as the opening act for
successful comics Buddy Hackett and Rodney
Dangerfield.

In 1983, Carrey headed west to Hollywood
where he starred in a made-for-television movie

called *Introducing…Janet*. Carrey's appearances on TV programs such as *The Duck Factory* and *Jim Carrey: Unnatural Act* (1991) led to a regular role on the hit comedy *In Living Color*.

Carrey's big screen debut came with 1984's *Finders Keepers*, but he didn't find success until he played the titular role in the 1994 comedy *Ace Ventura: Pet Detective*. From there, Carrey's expressive face, expert mimicry skills and physical brand of comedy kept the hits coming. He followed with *The Mask* (1994), *Dumb and Dumber* (1994), *Ace Ventura: When Nature Calls* (1995), *Batman Forever* (1995), *The Cable Guy* (1996) and *Liar Liar* (1997).

Jim had a rough start in life though. In his early years at school he describes himself as quiet and having no friends. Yet, he discovered that he could make friends by making people laugh. That was his turning point.

But the results weren't all positive. One teacher wrote on his report card: "Jim finishes his work first and then disrupts the class."

At home, he thoroughly enjoyed making faces and mimicking in his mirror.

His ambition showed when he began to think beyond entertaining his fellow students. At age ten he sent his resume to actress/comedienne Carol Burnett, hoping to be discovered.

It wasn't all up hill for Jim though. First, he had to work around his learning disability, dyslexia, in order to succeed in school. He did this by developing a phenomenal memory.

Although his dad tended to encourage his craziness, his mom was alarmed and often sent him to his room. No problem–just more time to practice in front of the mirror.

Money was another hurdle. His family lived in a rough district with lots of low-rent townhouses. By the tenth grade, he was trying to juggle eight-hour night shifts at the factory with school during the day. He was so exhausted that he couldn't understand what his teachers were talking about.

Jim didn't have any friends at school and feared that anyone getting close might discover his embarrassing poverty. With little learning and no relationships, he felt that school was getting him nowhere. He called it quits at 16.

Jim's family decided that their surroundings were taking them the wrong direction, so they packed up and moved to Canada with no job in sight. His parents and two siblings lived in a beat-up yellow Volkswagen camper van for a full eight months, parking in campgrounds.

You can imagine his emotional baggage–the loss of his teen years, feeling intellectually backwards, the embarrassment and hardship of poverty. Yet, perhaps that feeling of inferiority paved the way to his success by making him feel that he had to try harder than others. As one biographer wrote:

> "His greatest bursts of creativity were born out of desperation; so was his remarkable willingness to take risks."

His first public performance was in Toronto's Yuk-Yuk Comedy Club. Eleanor Goldhar, publicist for the club, noticed Jim's intensity. When he wasn't performing, he was quiet compared to the other comedians. In her own words,

> "You could see him watching and listening–observing closely, paying attention to

everything that was going on."

Jim says that he's always believed in magic. When he wasn't doing anything in Hollywood, he would drive up and sit in his car on Mulholland Drive, look out at the city, stretch out his arms, and say, "Everyone wants to work with me. I'm a really good actor. I have all kinds of great movie offers."

He would just repeat these things over and over, literally convincing himself that he had a couple of movies lined up. He'd drive down that hill, ready to take the world on, going, "Movie offers are out there for me, I just don't hear them yet."

He now reflects that it was like total affirmations, antidotes to the hardships that stemmed from his family background.

Around 1990, when Jim Carrey was a struggling young Canadian comic trying to make his way in Los Angeles, he drove his old Toyota up to Mulholland Drive.

While sitting there looking at the city below and dreaming of his future, he wrote himself a check for $10 million, dated it Thanksgiving 1995, added the notation "for acting services rendered," and carried it in his wallet from that day forth.

The rest, as they say, is history. Carrey's optimism and tenacity eventually paid off, and by 1995, after the huge box office success of *Ace Ventura: Pet Detective*, *The Mask*, and *Dumb and Dumber*, his asking price had risen to $20 million per picture.

When Carrey's father died in 1994, he placed the $10 million check into his father's coffin as a tribute to the man who had both started and nurtured his dreams of being a star.

What Is An Affirmation?

Okay, the best thing to do right now is give you the basic definition of an affirmation.

An affirmation is a statement you make to yourself, consciously or subconsciously, that will either empower you or disempower you.

The statement is usually preceded with "I am."

Positive affirmations are basically verbal, mental, or even physical reminders that life is inherently good, and that we can let go of our caveman tendencies. With positive affirmations, we recognize the values surrounding our lives, and we have reason to hope.

However, positive affirmations are so much more than that—they literally determine what actions we take, what thoughts we think, and what values we have. This is because they are inherently linked to our beliefs.

You have been using affirmations all your life! How many times have you said to yourself and others around you:

- I'm no good at that!
- I can't do that!
- I am not very intelligent!
- I am not good looking!
- I wish I was more like them!
- When I have money, I will…!

These are all examples of negative affirmations, and we all use them on a daily basis in one form or another. Your self-talk determines the beliefs you will have about yourself, about others, and about the world around you.

The affirmations you use in everyday life, whether subconscious or not, determine your beliefs and it's your beliefs that will ultimately decide how successful you are going to be in any area of your life.

How Do Positive Affirmations Work?

Positive affirmations basically work by retraining your brain to believe something new or to delete an old belief that you already hold about yourself. Using the belief formula in this book, an old belief can be questioned, to make that belief "molten." When we question our beliefs, they automatically lose a little power. However, we start to layer a new belief on top of our old belief, we find evidence to support it, and repeat it often. Given enough time, the new belief will become a rock-solid belief.

This is when positive affirmations come in. The affirmation process goes through a series of steps, something like this:

- State the affirmation.
- Creates energy to change your thoughts.

- Creates enough momentum to get over the dissonance barrier.
- Creates energy to change your actions.
- Creates energy to change your habits.
- Creates energy to change your reality.

Your Future Is Not In Front Of You

When we first start to look at affirmations, we generally think about the things we want in life and start with affirmations that will bring us what we want. So we think about having things in the future.

Affirmations are created to change your energy, not to bring the things you think you need into your life sometime in the future. When you change your energy, you bring things into your life that weren't there before, "good" or "bad."

We tend to think of the future as being somewhere in front of us, but I believe the future is all around you, and you are either moving closer to it or away from it, whether in front of you, at the side of you, above or below you, or in another dimension.

Changing your energy by using an affirmation

brings you closer to the "future" that you want— but it's actually bringing you closer to another reality. That might bake your noodle a little bit, so think about it like this:

In 2018, we wanted to buy a property in the West End of Glasgow, as I mentioned wanting one back in the late-90's, but there was no way it was going to happen. I repeated an affirmation in my mind, "We will find a way to buy a flat in the West End."

Notice I didn't affirm that "We now own a flat in the West End." If I had said that affirmation, it would have always reminded me that I didn't have a flat in the West End, which creates an energy of lack.

When I repeat the affirmation "We will find a way to buy a flat in the West End," it creates an energy of action, an energy of hope, and an energy of excitement. So when I repeated that affirmation, it brought our future closer to us by helping us to create actions and ideas in order to make buying a flat in the West End possible.

We bought our flat in the West End in March 2019. The funny thing was that we had to sell our existing house for a precise figure, or we would not be able to afford the new flat, and we needed the owners of the new flat to accept an exact price from us or we would not be able to afford it.

We sold our house for around £15,000 more than we thought we would sell it for (the exact price we needed), and we put an offer in for the new flat at home report price (this never usually happens in the West End, as the apartments go for around 10–15 percent higher).

We brought our "future" (another reality) closer to us with the affirmations we used, consciously and subconsciously. If I had not used the affirmation, our reality, that particular one, wouldn't have happened until much later, if at all.

So when you think about the things you want in life and think about the past, present, and future, it's not about thinking in the past, present, or future—it's about thinking about the different realities you are living in, have lived in, and want to live in.

With this in mind, we can start to look at

affirmations from another point of view and truly start to see their power. We will look at affirmations from now on as energy attractors.

CHAPTER SUMMARY

———

- The story of Jim Carrey and how affirmations helped him to become hugely successful.

- An affirmation is a statement you make to yourself, consciously or subconsciously, that will either empower you or disempower you. The statement is usually preceded with, "I am."

- Positive affirmations basically work by retraining your brain to believe something new or to delete an old belief that you already hold about yourself.

- Your future is not necessarily in front of you, it is all around you and you are either pulling your future closer to you or pushing it further away from you.

The Belief Principle

CHAPTER 16

The Seven Principles
Of Affirmation

*"Belief consists in accepting the affirmations of
the soul; unbelief, in denying them."*

RALPH WALDO EMERSON

Principle No. 1: Identify a reality

As you read above, affirmations are really about
attracting another reality to you, so you have to
first decide which reality you want to bring into
your life.

Do you want the reality of living in a new home?
Do you want the reality of having an amazing
partner in your life? Do you want the reality of
having an extra $100,000 in your life?

This is the fun part of affirmations, as you get to

decide which realities you want in your life.

If you're new to this or don't quite have the belief that I have in affirmations and how they work, start with something small.

So go ahead and think about having another $50 per month in your life.

Principle No. 2: Create an affirmation

Now that you have decided on some realities you'd like in your life, it's time to create an affirmation for each reality.

What's important about the affirmation you create is the feelings you have when you say it. It can be present or future tense; as I said before, there is no past, present, and future, only other realities, so it doesn't matter which tense is used.

So if you want a reality where you have more money, create an affirmation like: "I am attracting more money into my life every day," "I have more money in my life" or "Every day, money flows to me easily."

You get the picture. Make sure the words are powerful for you and use the ones above as guides. For each affirmation, repeat it every single day and often.

As I mentioned before, you tend to repeat the same thoughts over and over every single day anyway, so why not replace those thoughts with positive affirmations which will change you in ways you can't even imagine?

What I would do is take twenty-four minutes every morning to repeat a series of affirmations for the realities you want to see in your life.

So look at every area of your life and create an affirmation for a particular reality you want to happen in each.

Repeat these affirmations over and over for twenty-four minutes in the morning, preferably before sunrise so the universal energy force is much stronger.

Then throughout the day, repeat the affirmations whenever you get some spare thinking time (trust me, you have a lot of spare thinking time).

Principle No. 3: Breaking through the dissonance barrier

Now, what will happen is that your brain will turn to you and say, "Hey, numb nuts, this affirmation that you want another $10,000 per year is never going to happen, so stop saying it."

That's called cognitive dissonance, whereby you cannot hold two opposing beliefs at the same time. You have to ride through this period and keep on going with the affirmations while taking action to make the affirmation and new reality happen.

This uneasy dissonant feeling will eventually pass as your brain starts to accept that an extra $10,000 per year is coming to you very soon.

Principle No. 4: Change your thoughts

The more you persevere and continue doing the affirmations, the more your thoughts will navigate towards the new reality you are trying to create. When you first start an affirmation for a new reality, your thoughts start to grow the branches I was talking about earlier, and they start to develop more leaves, then eventually will form a trunk and then a root.

Your thoughts are powerful energy creators, so you have to be careful what you think. If you consciously design your own thoughts, you will be creating what seems like magic in your life.

Life just becomes a whole lot easier when you consciously take control of your thoughts, but it's a constant exercise to control them until eventually you'll automatically have control over them. Then, it will feel strange to turn control back over to your subconscious mind.

Principle No. 5: Change your actions

When you change your thoughts, you will start to notice you take more action to achieve the realities you want in your life.

This is the real power of affirmations. A lot of people think they can repeat an affirmation and sit on their backside and wait for their new reality to appear, but it doesn't work like that at all. It's all about taking action.

The affirmations that you are repeating will

eventually get you to take action as you are changing your thought environment on a daily basis.

You might think this is revolutionary, but it's the way you were meant to live.

You are simply reclaiming control over your own life.

Principle No. 6: Change your belief

When you change your thoughts and actions, you will eventually start to form new, more empowering beliefs.

These beliefs will become the core of who you are. You will truly start to believe in yourself like you've never believed before, and you will scarcely believe just how much power you really have over your life.

Your beliefs hold the power to truly change your life, and when you install the beliefs, they become a part of who you are.

This is why choosing your affirmations wisely and thoughtfully is so important.

Principle No. 7: The affirmation loop

With the repetition of positive affirmations, you can choose which beliefs you want to have about yourself.

Once you finally believe in these positive affirmations, you can start focusing on the grand scheme of what you want to do with your life. After you start taking steps to improve your life, you create positive feedback loops because all of a sudden, the values stated in the positive affirmations become more present in your life, making it easier and easier to have the energy to continue on your positive journey through this life.

You will realize just how powerful you are and just how amazing life is. Why do we NEED positive affirmations?

It's not that we need positive affirmations. It's more to do with becoming aware of our old affirmations and choosing the ones we want to have in our lives in order to change the limiting beliefs we have and to install new beliefs about ourselves.

CHAPTER SUMMARY

- The seven principles of affirmations…

    1. Identify a reality.
    2. Create an affirmation.
    3. Break through the dissonance barrier.
    4. Change your thoughts.
    5. Change your actions.
    6. Change your beliefs.
    7. The affirmation loop.

PART 2

——

KNOWING THE BELIEFS YOU HAVE AND CHANGING ALL THE RULES

CHAPTER 17

The Belief Formula

*"If I do not believe as you believe, it proves that
you do not believe as I believe, and that
is all that it proves."*

THOMAS PAINE

I have come up with a belief formula based on
my years of studying this, and it's a simple one.
The belief formula is:

Perception + Evidence + Repetition + Time = Belief

Now, to illustrate this formula, I'd like to tell you
a story about a girl named Sharon who is
twenty-two years old. Sharon has never really
believed that she is attractive, which is
reflective of a lot of people in the world today,
both female and male.

One day while at work, a male friend paid her a

compliment and said she looked really good and "hot." This took Sharon by surprise, but she didn't really think any more about it. However, when she went home that night, she looked in the mirror and thought about what her friend had said. And she thought that she was actually looking a bit better than she had been.

A few nights later, when she was out with friends, she was approached by a good-looking guy who asked if he could buy her a drink. Sharon was really flattered but politely refused to take the drink, which caused a little stir among her friends, who joked with her about this. Again, she was taken aback by this compliment.

Sharon started to reflect on recent events and began to question and challenge her perception of her beliefs about herself. Other small things like this happened over the next few weeks, and Sharon's (self) belief started to take hold.

A few weeks later, Sharon was out shopping by herself, and she saw a nice pair of jeans and decided to try them on. She looked in the mirror in the changing room (which as you know can be traumatic for anyone!) and was able to recognize that she actually looked good.

And she acknowledged that she liked what she saw in the mirror.

This was the formation of a new belief about herself. A few weeks later, her mother said to her that over the past few months there had been a marked difference in her appearance, and she was looking wonderful. Now, it was unusual for her mother to pay her a compliment, but she was able to take this compliment in the positive manner in which it had been offered. So Sharon was able to take this belief obtained in the previous few months and let it set in her mind. Sharon had now formed the belief that she was attractive.

Due to the formation of this belief, which had been reinforced by the compliments of others, Sharon started to act, dress, and even walk differently. This was all a result of her newfound belief in herself. She began to dress to accentuate her best assets, and she went to the gym to maintain her attractive figure.

This change affected her thoughts, and she started thinking more positively confidently.

She began to take on bigger challenges in life.

The example of Sharon and her new belief is a rather crude example of how beliefs can be installed at an unconscious level. However, the purpose of this whole book is to consciously install new beliefs.

So let's look at the belief formula again and break it down and find out how to install a new belief. We will dive much deeper into this, so this is a brief overview:

Perception + Evidence + Repetition + Time = Belief

Perception. This is a view you would like to have about yourself, one that you might currently not have, e.g., I am intelligent. If you currently have the belief you are not intelligent and you'd like to change that, you first have to acknowledge the belief that you want to install: "I am intelligent."

Evidence. Once you have told yourself a few times, I am intelligent, you will then start to look for evidence of this in your history. You will be able to find evidence—it's just a matter of taking the time to look for it.

Repetition. When you first want to install a new belief, it has to be repeated in various ways. So whenever you do something you view as being the action of someone intelligent, you tell yourself, I am intelligent. You do this every single time and repeat it often. However, it's not just about repeating it over and over—it's about repeating it when you find the evidence.

Time. When you have spent some time gathering and storing evidence that you are intelligent, it will quickly become a rock-solid belief.

Belief Shift. Changing beliefs doesn't happen overnight. Your current beliefs have taken you years to form and can often be such solid beliefs that it is difficult to change them. So please understand that this belief shift will not happen within a few days, except when you have an epiphany belief change, but you will start to see the results within a few weeks.

Imagine you have a rock-solid belief that you are not intelligent, and you've had this most of your life. The very first thing you do is start to question that belief and ask, "Is this really true?"

When you do that, the rock that is your belief will start the process of becoming molten. Then, as you use the belief formula process, that state of solidity will become more and more molten until your old belief melts away and a new belief, I am intelligent, takes its place. That's when the new belief will become rock-solid.

Cognitive Dissonance

Something happens in your brain when you try to install a new empowering belief over an old limiting belief, and it's called *cognitive dissonance*.

Cognitive dissonance states that you cannot hold two opposing beliefs in your mind at the same time, e.g., I am not intelligent, and I am intelligent. These are two opposing beliefs, and one of them will win out. So you have to be aware that when you tell yourself, I am intelligent, your mind will try to reject that belief, as it already holds the opposite belief.

This is overcome by using the belief formula above and why I say that this doesn't usually happen overnight.

There are a few caveats to this.

The Epiphany Belief Changer

At the beginning of the book, I mentioned that I had a realization one day while walking home from school that I am intelligent. The belief that I was not intelligent had stuck with me for more than a decade and was literally changed in one moment of epiphany. A lot of people have had these moments in their lives, and it can change an old limiting belief in an instant.

An epiphany is when you have a deep insight into something that goes way beyond just understanding it or comprehending it. When I had this, one of my many epiphany moments, I understood and comprehended that I must be intelligent long before I truly believed I was.

With an epiphany moment, something clicks into place inside your mind and you are instantly transformed. My epiphany moment changed my life in a huge way, and the effects are still being felt today—and that is just one belief.

The extremely powerful *epiphany belief changer*

is the only instance when an old belief can change in an instant, and it can happen in a variety of ways.

Think about the Charles Dickens book *A Christmas Carol*, where the main character, Scrooge, has an epiphany in one night. Previously, he was a miserly, bitter, twisted man who didn't treat people well at all.

That night, the ghosts of Christmas past, present, and future gave him a much deeper understanding of why he was the way he was and the effect that he was having on people around him.

In these moments, a deep understanding occurred; Scrooge had an epiphany and realized he didn't want to be the miserly old man he had been. Instead, he wanted joy and kindness in his life. We all know what happened when he had this epiphany.

These epiphany moments don't happen often, but when they do, they are life-changing.

I hope with this book you have at least one epiphany moment so you can experience the power it has on your life. In fact, I would be a little disappointed if you didn't have an epiphany moment, so let me know on social media if you do *#TBPEpiphanyMoment*.

Having said that, even if you don't have an epiphany moment while reading this book, you will be able to completely change your beliefs. This is not a competition. Your life will be changed if you put in a little effort and work on the program I'm laying out for you.

CHAPTER SUMMARY

———

- The Belief Formula: Perception + Evidence + Repetition + Time = Belief.

- Belief shift. Usually beliefs do not change overnight, however, on rare occasions they can. They usually happen over time.

- The epiphany belief change is a rare instant belief shift.

- Cognitive dissonance states that you can hold two opposing beliefs in your mind at the same time.

CHAPTER 18

Update Your Belief Stories

"Stories can conquer fear, you know. They can make the heart bigger."

BEN OKRI

Throughout your whole life, you have gathered beliefs either to carry like a burden or to guide you happily into your future. What you also gather at the same time are the stories that accompany each of these beliefs.

Let me give you an example:

During a conversation with a young woman who has relationship issues and who keeps on picking men who do not treat her well, she reveals that her father was a serial womanizer who treated her mother like crap, mentally and financially torturing her, which can be just as bad as physical torture; abuse of any kind is still abuse.

The woman goes on to say that she knew her father was not a good husband to her mother, but she knew he loved her and her siblings. When she grew up, she found she was unconsciously attracted to men with the same behaviors as her father.

She was constantly fighting with her partners and constantly disappointed in her inability to form a deep relationship. Consequently, she developed the belief that "all men are... (not very nice)."

When it was pointed out to this young woman that in actuality all the men she chose were not nice, there was a long silence as this statement was processed.

This woman had carried the belief story that all men behaved like her father, and if they didn't behave that way, they weren't real men. In other words, the "nice" guys were dismissed as not being real men, despite her knowing that her father's behavior was not acceptable.

Update Your Belief Stories

When digging deep into this and helping her to reframe her belief and change her story about what a real man is, the belief then changes and ultimately helps her relationships. This story is not uncommon, and it illustrates how our stories need to be changed in order for us to move on in life.

A few weeks before I was due to publish this book, I received a question from a member on my Facebook page
www.facebook.com/changeyourthoughtstoday.

Q: Can you talk about why certain kind of woman attract the same guy's, with addictions, thanks.

A: The very short answer is: The reason men and women keep attracting the same kinds of people in their lives is down to a self worth issue. You attract the people you think you deserve in your life and this is a subconscious thing.

It's not about working on anything else other than your self worth and self esteem. Once you truly believe, deep down, that you are worth so much more than the type of men you are attracting, you will start to see different types of people coming into your life.

We all have stories that we are carrying with us like baggage through our various different paths in life, and it's up to us to change those stories.

We can't keep blaming the past or our parents for the way we are. We are responsible for the way we are, and we are responsible for the beliefs we hold. This book shows you that you get to choose your beliefs. I'm not saying it's easy to let go of the past, but it can definitely be done. It is your responsibility to help yourself.

Now, I know that this is not going to sit well with a lot of you, and you'll come up with all the excuses to absolve yourself of blame for the way you are, but I have to say again: it's time to change your story. If you don't, you're going to go through life annoyed and angry, and you will never have power over your own life.

When you have the power to own your life and everything you do, life becomes immeasurably easier.

This may sound counterintuitive, as you might think it takes strength and a lot of mental energy to develop the power to own your life, but it's much harder to keep forcing your way through life—forcing anything expends a lot more mental and spiritual energy.

How To Change Your Story

This one is simple to implement, but it's amazing how many people do not do it because it is too simple. There is a belief throughout the world that anything that is simple cannot work; it has to be hard for it to work.

People are addicted to the struggle. When they see something that is simple, they immediately dismiss it. You see, they mistake "simple" for "less powerful." Let me tell you something just now, and it's true for everything in life:

The simple solution is usually the most powerful.

I am going to give you some examples of how the simple way is the most powerful.

Which of these resonate with you?

- If you want to earn more money as a coach, simply double your fees.

- If you want to save up to $1,000 per year on your utilities, simply change your energy provider, insurance provider, and broadband provider every year.

- If you want to lose weight without doing too much, simply drink two liters of water every day.

- If you want to lose even more weight, simply stop eating bread altogether.

- If you want to write a book, simply write for ONLY five minutes per day, and you will have a 73,000-word book in one year.

- If you want a tidy house all the time, simply clean your house for fifteen minutes every day, and you won't have to spend two hours on the weekend doing it.

- If you want to get fit, simply take a walk every morning for fifteen minutes.

- If you want to gain strength, simply do thirty push-ups every day.

You get the picture. I could literally write a book about all the simple things you could do to change your life (in fact, look out for that book, as it may be coming to a store near you).

So, simple is powerful—repeat that phrase a few times and start looking for evidence to show that simple is powerful. When you do this, your mind will start to look for simple solutions to everything you do in life.

Okay, I digress. To change your story, simply change what you tell yourself and others on a daily basis. No massive change required—just change what you say about the thing you want to change.

As an example, the memory story:

A lot of people want to have a better memory, but how is that going to be possible when they tell themselves and others just how bad their memory is?

"Oh, I have a terrible memory, I'll never remember that." "I'm sorry, I have a terrible memory and can't remember your name." "I wish I had a better memory."

"My memory is getting worse all the time."

How on earth can you expect to have a good memory when you constantly tell yourself all of the above? Change what you say, and you change what you believe.

So you could change the above sentences to:

"I have an amazing memory."

"I will remember that easily."

"I've got a great memory for faces."

"My memory is improving all the time."

You might be saying, "Well, Steve, that will not work. It's not that simple."

It will and does work, and I know because the memory example was me around ten years ago.

I actually thought there was something wrong with me, my memory was so bad. However, when I changed the phrases that I used surrounding my memory, I changed the story and subsequently changed my belief to one of having an amazing memory.

Did it help me? 100 percent. My wife often comments about how good my memory for numbers is.

So when you have a belief that you need to change, look at the old story you've been telling your whole life, and then start to change your story by changing the phrases you use surrounding that story.

CHAPTER SUMMARY

- Your belief story is the story surrounding particular beliefs that you hold about yourself.

- Changing your story can be extremely simple and very effective.

- Some examples of easy stories to change with strategies that help you change your belief story.

CHAPTER 19

What Are Your Current Beliefs?

"Where you are right now in your life is down to all the beliefs you have accumulated. If you want to change where you are, start changing some of your beliefs."

STEVEN AITCHISON

It might seem like a strange question to ask, but I'm going to ask anyway:

What beliefs do you hold about yourself?

I'll give you a few minutes to think about that one, as it's a little trickier than you might first imagine.

Tricky, isn't it!

Slave Or Master?

The reason we find it so difficult is that we rarely pay attention to the beliefs we have. However, we have to recognize that either we are a slave to our beliefs, or we are a master of them.

If you were to master just a few of your beliefs, your life would change beyond measure. Imagine if you managed to install a new belief that you are a supremely confident person. How do you think this one belief would change your life? It would change it in every way.

Simply understanding and mastering your beliefs is going to bring about a massive shift in your life.

Uncover Your Beliefs

You've learned the theory of beliefs, how they are formed, why we have them, what role they serve in our lives, and the rules that come from our beliefs.

Now it's time for the good stuff, the stuff that truly helps us to transform our lives.

It's time to break all the rules.

Okay, so I want to give you the first practical exercise of this book to help you out with uncovering your beliefs. This is going to open your eyes, amaze you, and give you huge insights into your own life that you may not have thought about before.

The Belief Wheel

No doubt you will have seen something similar to this called the *Wheel of Life*, which is used a lot in life coaching.

We are going to break your life up into eight sections.

I first started using the *Wheel of Life* when I attended a seminar by Jack Black (no, not the movie star!) about fifteen years ago.

I found it extremely useful to have a visual representation of where my life was at a particular moment in time.

On the next page, there is an example of a *Wheel of Life*:

What Are Your Current Beliefs?

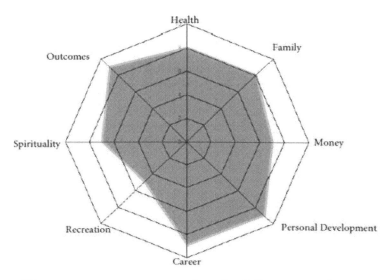

The gray area represents all of the areas in our lives. It lets us see immediately what areas we might want to focus on more.

The example above shows us that "Recreation" is out of balance with other life areas.

Your exercise for today:

Part One

I'd like you to take ten minutes to think about the eight major areas of your life and give each one a score out of ten, with one being the least satisfied and ten being the most satisfied.

As you think about each area of your life, ask yourself:

- How well am I doing in this area of my life?
- Is there room for improvement?
- How satisfied am I with how this area of my life is going?

___ **Health.** This has to do with how healthy you are at the moment: Do you get enough exercise, do you have any detrimental habits that could harm you, do you eat well, do you have a lot of energy, and are you stressed?

___ **Family.** How is your family life right now? Do you spend enough time with your family, do you make time for special days, is it quality time you spend with them, and do you call up family often?

___ **Money.** How are your finances at the moment? Do you have savings, do you live from month to month, do you have plans in place for the future, and do you have a lot of debt?

___ **Personal development.** Are you spending time on your own development? Do you spend time improving your mind with activities, reading books, going to seminars, participating in online courses, and feeding your mind with quality information?

___ **Career.** Are you satisfied with your chosen career path? Do you like your job, could you do more at work to feel satisfied, are you studying the right course at university or college to get you to where you want to be, and are you spending too much time at work?

___ **Recreation.** Do you spend enough time doing the things you enjoy in life? Do you watch too much TV, do you read a lot, do you get out of the house enough, and do you spend recreation time with your kids or family?

___ **Spirituality.** How is your spiritual life? This does not necessarily have to relate to religion— it has more to do with feeding your soul, your spirit. Are you getting enough joy into your life? Are you inspired?

___ **Outcomes.** Do you have aspirations for the future? Are you actively working towards them? What are they?

The trick to doing this is to listen to your instincts and try not to overthink the score. You will think of a score for your area and immediately get a feel for whether that score truly represents that particular area of your life. There is no point in pretending that an area of your life is going okay by assigning it a high score if you know there is a lot of improvement needed in that area.

Be honest with yourself and admit that there might be issues in that area. That is what we are going to rectify with this course, so be as honest as possible, as only you will see your scores.

Part Two

Now for the second part of this exercise. Think about what is holding you back from having a score of ten in each of the areas.

For example, you might say for recreation: "I don't have enough time," "I'm too busy," "other areas are more important," or "I don't have the energy."

With the example above, you can easily see

that these are things you tell yourself. I used to tell myself that I had no time to go to the gym, and I was making myself believe that, which always prevented me from going. I do have time—what I don't have is my priorities in order. I valued my health but not as much as I valued my work, and my family, money, or anything else.

So I created a new belief that I do have time for my health and set that belief up to make it extremely important. Without my health, my family time suffers, my ability to make an income suffers, and my work suffers—so it's about setting up your beliefs and setting up your priorities.

So you see, by saying simple things like "Oh, I don't really have the time to do that," you are creating a belief that prevents you from doing the very thing you need to do.

Go through all the areas of your life and ask yourself why you haven't scored a ten in each area, and you'll discover the beliefs that are currently holding you back in general.

Now, I am not saying you need to score a ten in

each of the areas; that's not practical, not necessary, and not realistic. Your *Wheel of Life* is not about having a perfectly balanced life, as there really is no such thing.

That may sound odd to hear, as we have heard so much about work-life balance, but what it's really about is working with what you have to do and making the most of what you want to do. We'll talk more about this later.

To give you another example in your life, you might look at your "Spirituality" and intuitively feel that you have a score of six because you neglect your spiritual side for other areas of your life.

Some of your beliefs about why you neglect the spiritual side of you might be:

- I don't have time.
- It's not as important as other areas of my life.
- I am not really a spiritual person.
- I am too busy.

CHAPTER SUMMARY

———

- Part One of the belief wheel exercise is to discover your current beliefs in all areas of your life.

- Part Two of the exercise is to ask why you haven't scored a 10 in each area of your life.

PART 3

———

THE DEEP SOUL FEELING
METHOD

CHAPTER 20

The Deep Soul Feeling Method

"The soul is placed in the body like a rough diamond, and must be polished, or the luster of it will never appear."

DANIEL DEFOE

During the course of writing this book, I kept asking my subconscious mind, what simple exercises, rituals and affirmations could I give you to truly empower you and to help you change your beliefs quickly and easily, by creating a routine that you do every single morning.

After my morning run at about 6:00AM, I take a walk and sit and meditate at Glasgow University grounds. It's a beautiful spot where I am facing a beautiful 19th-century gothic-style wing of the

215

university building that reminds me of Hogwarts.

As I sit on a park-style bench with my eyes closed, the phrase, "I am the light, I am the energy, I am the love, I am the universe" comes to me.

I am not a religious person in any way, but I love the sound of this phrase and sit there for the next fifteen minutes repeating the phrase over and over and feeling the words.

It is extremely calming, comforting, and empowering.

When I open my eyes, I know I have one of the main exercises that I have been seeking.

That question to my subconscious mind brought a lot of cool new ideas for this book.

One of them was the *Deep Soul Feeling Method* which consists of a four-part ritual that is really simple and yet extremely powerful.

For the next three weeks, I sat for fifteen minutes per day repeating the mantra:

I am the light
I am the energy
I am the love
I am the universe

It was extremely empowering, and I felt lighter, spiritually and emotionally—so much so that I have incorporated it into my daily routine. It gives me a lot of strength. My internal energy has changed, and I am truly attracting more of the things I want in my life without having to think too much about them.

Now it is time to hand it over to you and incorporate belief change with these empowering mantras, and routines.

Here is the result: *The Deep Soul Feeling Method*.

The Deep Soul Feeling Method

In part four of this book, I have identified seven beliefs that will completely transform your life when you work on them and make them a part of your life. They will change literally every area of your life from your health to your wealth.

For each of the seven beliefs in part four, there are extremely powerful exercises to do. For this it would be great if you had a brand-new unused notebook to use as a journal, of sorts. Trust me when I say that writing down these exercises in a journal will make the installation of new beliefs so much quicker.

We are going to use the *Deep Soul Feeling Method* to work on all seven of these beliefs.

A word of warning: you may get emotional while performing the exercises in this section. This is perfectly natural, as it is releasing blocked up energy that has been in your body for years.

I encourage you to share your experiences with the Facebook group, so you're not left hanging with no one to talk to about the emotional release you feel.

There are four parts to the *Deep Soul Feeling Method*:

1. Writing down the belief.
2. The mantra.
3. The installation of the belief.
4. Making it a rock-solid belief.

When you have read each of the seven beliefs, come back to this section of the book to install the new belief and do the short, simple exercises that follow.

Preparation

Please see the resources section to watch a video on how to do this.

- Buy a quality A4 lined notebook, like a Pukka Pad with 200 or 250 pages. This is going to be your *Belief Principle Journal*.

- Open the front cover and on the very first page in the middle just write the words: "Belief Principle Journal."

- On the next page on the very top line, centered and capitalized, write the word: "BELIEF."

- Underneath that line, centered and capitalized, write the belief you want to install, e.g., "I AM WORTHY."

Skip one line.

On the next line, to the left and capitalized, write the word: "MANTRA."

Skip 10 lines.

On the next line, to the left and capitalized, write the word: "EVIDENCE."

Underneath this line, in the margins, for each line write the numbers 1 to 22 (Or whoever many lines are left on the page).

That completes page one.

On the opposite page, page two:

On the very top line, centered and capitalized, write the word: "BELIEF."

Underneath that line, centered and capitalized, write the belief you want to install, e.g., "I AM WORTHY."

Skip one line.

On the next line, to the left and capitalized, write the word: "EVIDENCE."

Skip 10 lines.

Underneath this line, in the margins, for each line write the numbers 1 to 10.

Skip one line.

On the next line, to the left and capitalized, write the word: "THOUGHTS."

For the next four pages, copy what you did for page two.

That completes all of the preparatory work.

For each of the sections, here is the routine that you perform to start changing your beliefs and changing your life.

Pages 1-2

Every time you listen to the mantra MP3 for the corresponding belief, e.g., I am worthy, write down the belief on line one and then add a comma. Every time you listen to the mantra, write down the belief. So if you listen to it for 30 days, you will have written down "I am worthy" 30 times (about 6-8 times per line).

The Belief Principle

For the evidence section, you are going to think of as many pieces of evidence as you can to prove the belief and write each piece of evidence on one line (e.g. for the belief I am worthy):

1. I am a fantastic mother.
2. I am a kind and very caring person.
3. I think about other people's feelings.
4. I am good at my job.
5. I love learning.
6. I bring in money to pay the bills and do it with a good heart.

There are about 22 lines on the first page to write your evidence lines in.

The evidence section on page two is a continuation of page one and a space to write more evidence down either from your past, present or future (you will gather evidence from now on and write it in here).

The thoughts section on page two is for you to record your feelings, thoughts, and how you may have changed regarding this particular belief (e.g., I feel a bit silly writing in this book, but I realize for me to change I need to change what I am doing.

222

I actually didn't realize just how much evidence there is to show myself I am worthy. I am actually a pretty decent guy and writing these things down has helped me realize that).

Pages 3-6

These pages are exactly the same as page two. So as you find more evidence you will have space to continue recording that evidence.

You don't have to fill all six pages, but it will give you the space to do so if you need it.

You also just keep recording your thoughts on each page, so when you finish one page of thoughts, continue onto the next page.

Part One: Writing

With your brand new A4 notepad we are going to start to install your first belief or overwrite an old belief you have about yourself.

Hopefully, you've read the preparation work in the previous section so you will know exactly what to do here.

The Belief Principle

So, for the first belief it's time to write in your notepad what belief you wish to install. This is really important as we all have different modalities in which we learn and absorb information into our subconscious mind: In education, the four learning modalities are visual, auditory, kinesthetic, and tactile.

When we are writing it hits all four of these modalities if we say out loud as we are writing: "I am worthy."

That's it for now. It's now time to listen to the corresponding mantra or do the mantra exercise on your own (e.g., for the belief: I am worthy you can recite the mantra):

I am the light
I am the energy
I am the love
I am the universe
I am worthy

Do this for 10 minutes every day, preferably in the morning as it really sets you up for a brilliant day.

Every time you do one of these mantras, write

down the belief next to the mantra section in your notepad.

Part Two: The Mantra

For every belief you wish to change, starting with the seven mentioned in this book, you will be repeating this mantra with the affirmation of each belief at the end. As you sit in your quiet zone for fifteen minutes, place your hand over your heart area and repeat the mantra for each belief you are going to install.

Feel what you are saying. When you say, I am the light, feel the light shining through you and feel yourself being part of the light of the world; feel the energy of the world and you being a part of that; feel the love flowing through every part of your body; feel the universe inside you and you being a part of the universe.

So the first seven mantras will look like this:

I am the light
I am the energy
I am the love
I am the universe
I am worthy

I am the light
I am the energy
I am the love
I am the universe
I am responsible for everything that happens in my life

I am the light
I am the energy
I am the love
I am the universe
I have the ability to be wealthy

I am the light
I am the energy
I am the love
I am the universe
I am capable of anything

I am the light
I am the energy
I am the love
I am the universe
I am courageous

I am the light
I am the energy
I am the love

The Deep Soul Feeling Method

I am the universe
I never settle for second best

I am the light
I am the energy
I am the love
I am the universe
I am enough

It is important to try to feel the words of these mantras as you say them.

After ten minutes, put your arms by your side and take five minutes to think about how you felt as you carried out this exercise and how you felt saying each line.

That is round one of the *Deep Soul Feeling Method*, and the purpose is to gauge your own reactions to this belief.

What happens a lot of the time is that people will have a few different reactions such as:

- They feel comfortable saying this to themselves and feel happy to get back in touch with the feeling of the belief they are installing.

- It is very uncomfortable for them—nothing could be further from the truth, and they dismiss the feeling and the words.
- Some people will feel very emotional.
- For some, it's the first time they have heard that they are worthy or that they are capable of anything or any of the other beliefs.
- This is emotionally freeing but can also be difficult for some, as it brings up a lot of emotions.

Whatever you felt, you have freed some of the energy blockages within you—even if you felt anger.

If you wish, you can record your feelings about each of the exercises in your own *Belief Principle Journal*. By doing this, it releases more of the energy that comes with unblocking these emotions.

Part Three: The Installation Of The Belief

With each new belief you install, take note of the belief and start to write down evidence for why that particular belief is true.

For example:

The Deep Soul Feeling Method

Take the perception, I Am Worthy, and start to think about your life in general and jot down everything you have ever felt worthy about.

For example:

- I am a great mother/father.
- I am a great husband/wife.
- I am amazing at my job.
- I am very creative.
- I have great friends who respect me.
- I am in a loving, healthy relationship.
- I am tenacious.
- I get things done.
- I have done a lot for charity.
- I have completed a marathon.
- I graduated from university.

The more things you think about, the more will come to you. Write as much as you can in fifteen minutes. If you can't think of one single thing, let it go and let the thought marinate in your mind and something will bubble to the surface of your conscious mind. When that happens, record it in your journal.

So the above example shows you a lot of the things you have done in life that make you feel worthy as a human being, as a mother, as a father, as a husband/wife, as a friend, as a son/daughter, and as a sister/brother.

I am sure more and more examples will come up where you have felt worthy in your life, and that is brilliant. What you are doing in this part of the exercise is gathering evidence to prove to yourself that you are worthy, that you are capable of anything, and that you do have the ability to become wealthy, etc.

We now have the perception + evidence parts of the formula, and now we move to the repetition.

The repetition part comes with saying the mantra each morning as described above using the special mantra for each belief. The time part of the equation will come when you stick with the exercises for each of the seven beliefs for thirty days each.

If you are finding it difficult to install a particular belief, place your hand over your heart area and mentally repeat the mantra for that belief: I am the light, I am the energy, I am the love, I am the universe, (your new belief here).

Do this whenever you can, when you have spare thinking time, when you are in the queue at the supermarket, when you are driving and stuck in traffic, or when you are waiting on someone. The beauty is that this mantra can be repeated anytime and anywhere, and it doesn't take long at all.

Twenty-one to thirty days should be enough time for you to see a noticeable difference in the way you feel about yourself, and you will start to see the knock-on benefits of installing the new belief, in all areas of your life. You will feel more confident, more assertive, more creative, less apprehensive, and more decisive, and you will start to feel that you are taking control of your life instead of life—and others—controlling you.

After thirty days of the *Deep Soul Feeling Exercise* you no longer need to do the mantra every day; you can do a top-up every week to strengthen the belief even more.

However, what you will find is that you will still repeat, mentally, I am the light, I am the energy, I am the love, I am the universe, (insert new belief here) in the days, weeks, and months after doing your first thirty days.

Part Four: Making It A Rock-Solid Belief

One more thing to make each belief a rock-solid one for you is to mentally take note of every new situation where you have found evidence to prove your new belief.

Physically write it down and add it to the evidence list you wrote out earlier. This is extremely important, as it will make your belief a root belief instead of a leaf belief—so the belief will be a part of who you are and affect the trunk, branches, and leaves of your soul. In other words, it will become a deep part of who you are as a person.

PART 4

———

THE SEVEN BELIEFS THAT WILL TRANSFORM YOUR LIFE

CHAPTER 21

The Seven Beliefs That Will Transform Your Life

In this section, we are going to start the installation of the seven beliefs that will transform your life.

These seven beliefs are not the only beliefs to install. The seven major beliefs I am about to share with you will have an amazing impact on your life.

In fact, if you manage to install and take to heart only one or two of these beliefs, that will be enough to transform you in ways you cannot imagine.

However, don't stop at one or two go for all seven of the beliefs or come up with your own beliefs.

You can also share the beliefs with the community at:
www.TheBeliefPrinciple.com/FBGroup.

Belief No. 1: "I Am Worthy"

"When you get to a place where you understand that love and belonging, your worthiness, is a birthright and not something you have to earn, anything is possible."

BRENÉ BROWN

Every single person who has ever made it in life and is happy and confident believes they are worthy. When we don't believe we are worthy, that's when problems start to appear, and they stop us from moving forward.

What do I mean when I say "worthy"? It is obviously subjective, but we feel this in many areas in our lives. For example, in our relationships when we feel worthy of love and set positive boundaries, then the people we have relationships with know the boundaries and respect us. When we feel we are not worthy, we tend to let our boundaries slip, and people start to treat us like…well, let's just say they don't treat us with the respect we deserve.

We all know someone who commands respect from others and doesn't take any crap from anybody.

These people have set healthy boundaries because they know they are worthy of these boundaries.

However, it's not just relationships with other people that make us feel worthy. The relationships we have with ourselves can make us feel worthy or unworthy.

So it really depends on how you define feeling worthy and looking at the different areas of your life that make you feel worthy.

For example, you may feel 100 percent worthy as a mother or a father but may feel unworthy in your career.

The key is to feel worthy no matter what area of your life you are in. Knowing that you can never ever ever ever (get my point!) be perfect means you can and will feel worthy by doing your best in every area of your life.

We all have conversations with ourselves that will affirm our beliefs, negative or positive.

The conversations and belief statements of I Am Worthless.

- I will never amount to anything in my job; I'm just not good enough to move up.
- I always attract the wrong type of person in my relationships.
- I know my partner is going to leave me; I am just not good enough for them.
- I am nowhere near good enough to apply for that job.
- If I say "no" to someone, they might judge me.
- Why do I always think the worst is going to happen?
- Nobody really likes me, and to be honest, I don't blame them.
- This is all my fault; I always manage to mess things up.
- Just ignore me…
- My partner is always berating me when they give me advice.
- I feel stupid…
- Who the hell would even give me a second glance?

There are many more statements that people who feel worthless tell themselves, and I am sure you recognize some from your past or your present.

You can see how utterly disempowering they are. Just reading them brings your energy down, so imagine how you would feel if you constantly affirmed these statements day in and day out.

Well, we're going to change all that, and it's the first belief that you will install in your life in order to feel amazing again—or maybe for the first time.

In contrast to the list of statements above and the conversations we have with ourselves when we feel completely unworthy, I want to show you the other side and share with you the energy of reading statements of feeling worthy.

The conversations and statements of I Am Worthy…

- I have as good a chance as anybody else when I apply for that job.

- I set healthy boundaries in my relationships, and I respect their boundaries; I seem to exude that energy and have amazing relationships.
- I will never settle for second best in anything in my life.
- My partner is lucky to have me as a partner, and I am lucky to have them.
- Having the courage to say, "no" when required is empowering and shows others I am not a pushover.
- I don't need the acceptance of others to make me feel worthy.
- If someone doesn't like me, I am not responsible for their feelings toward me.
- I am willing and able to put my mind to anything if I really want it.
- I deserve all the success I have in this life as long as I put in the time and the effort.

Do you feel the difference in the energy of the statements above as opposed to the previous statements?

They are empowering, aren't they? They lift you up and inspire you to keep going and be the best you can be.

Now it is time to go and install the belief using the *Deep Soul Feeling Method* described in part three of this book.

Belief No. 2: I Am Responsible For Everything That Happens In My Life

"If you're sitting around waiting on somebody to save you, to fix you, to even help you, you are wasting your time because only you have the power to take responsibility to move your life forward."

OPRAH WINFREY

WARNING: This section of the book contains advice that might seriously annoy you.

I always get a little flak when I tell clients to take responsibility for everything in their lives. If you don't take responsibility for your life, then you are giving away your power to other people and telling yourself that you don't control your life. Have the courage to take responsibility.

When I was an addiction counselor and clients told me they had an alcohol addiction, the inevitable question would come up:

The Belief Principle

Why do you drink?

A lot of clients would say they drink because they are addicted to alcohol and don't know how to stop, but a large proportion of clients would say they drink because of something that happened in their past, or they drink because they don't have much in life, or because their wife left them, or because they are bankrupt.

Alcoholics drink because they choose to drink.

Drug addicts take drugs because they choose to take drugs. Gamblers gamble because they choose to gamble. Yes, it's an addiction, and the compulsion to do all these things mentioned is strong, but it's still a choice.

I was a smoker, and there was always a choice before I put the first cigarette of the morning to my lips:

I had the choice not to smoke or to smoke.

When we strip away all the beliefs, the societal consciousness surrounding addiction, all the "health" terms surrounding addiction, then we are left with two things: a choice of yes or no.

However, we also choose to do the good things in life. Writers write because they choose to write. Teachers teach because they choose to teach.

There is no outside force that makes us do what we do in life, and it's going to be hard to hear these words if you feel your life is in a bit of a mess just now.

In the alcohol counseling sessions I carried out, if we could get to the stage when the client would take responsibility for their drinking, their chances of giving up alcohol increased massively.

Similarly, we have to take responsibility for every aspect of our life; only then can we take actions to change it.

If we are in a crappy job, we should take responsibility and tell ourselves we are choosing to be in this crappy job and then find a less crappy job and leave the other one.

If you immediately said, "But..." in your head when you read that sentence, then you are living your current inner scripts.

If you are in a crappy relationship, take responsibility and say, "I am choosing to be in this crappy relationship."

When you do that, you are a little more enlightened and choose to no longer stay in the crappy relationship.

If you said, "Yes, Steve, but..." then you are living your current inner scripts.

If you don't have enough money in your life, you have chosen to not have enough money due to the old beliefs you had about money (by the way, that's going to start to change by the end of this book). If I said to you that your life literally depended on you earning an extra £33 per day, would you find a way to make an extra £33 per day?

Of course you would, and yet we still complain that there's not enough money in our lives. £33 per day is around £12,000 per year, and just think how much of a difference that would make. In fact, just asking that question every day for thirty days would dramatically increase your chances of more money coming into your life.

We need to get off the "poor me" train, take responsibility, and give ourselves a good kick up the arse.

Now, I know all of that sounds a little like I am being arrogant and telling you off, but someone's gotta tell you at some point, and it may as well be me.

If you've not fallen out with me, then please read on. If you have gone off in a huff and thought, "You arrogant little (insert expletive here)," then put this book down, stew for a few hours, and then come back to this book knowing that what I say is said with love.

The conversations and statements of being a victim…

- It's not my fault.
- Why does it always happen to me.
- You make me feel angry.
- I am always getting picked on I can't do it because…
- The future doesn't look great.
- The world is not a good place to live.
- I wouldn't bring children into a world like this.

The conversations and statements of I Am Responsible For Everything That Happens In My Life...

- I have complete control over my life.
- I know what I want.
- I am confident.
- I believe in myself.
- I am strong and powerful.
- I am assertive.
- I feel great about myself and life.
- I am optimistic about the future.

What Is Responsibility?

We are going to see responsibility as something slightly different from the conventional meaning which is "the state or fact of being accountable or to blame for something." We are going to view responsibility as:

Your ability to respond to the situations and people in your life.

This is a conscious choice and should not be mistaken for the ability to react to something, which is an unconscious choice.

I believe we are put on this earth to reach our full potential within the confines of physical laws. What we learn along the way should then be shared with others in order for a new generation to outgrow our experiences and take our learning, and teaching, to a higher level.

The universe sends you challenges in life to strengthen your ability to respond. The stronger you become, the bigger the challenges will be and the bigger the rewards will, whatever reward system you think is appropriate.

Usually the reward system is financial; however, as we grow, we will no longer see money as a reward—we will view it as a natural resource that everyone has access to, and therefore the reward system will become less significant.

What we also have to remember is that we are not responsible for anybody else in life. If the universe is sending you challenges in order to strengthen your ability to respond, it is also sending everyone else challenges.

So please do not dishonor someone by feeling responsible for them.

You might be thinking, "But Steve, I have a responsibility for my children…" and you would be right, but it is not to respond for your children.

Your responsibility is to empower and help your children develop their own abilities to respond to the world and the people who reside in it.

By taking responsibility for yourself, you ensure that you are fit and healthy emotionally, physically, mentally, and spiritually. If you are in that space, fully fit and healthy, and you have surplus energy, then you may help others empower themselves to learn to be responsible.

At the beginning of this chapter, I wrote that we need to "get off the poor me train and take responsibility for our own life."

Normally I am not that abrupt, but I deliberately made that statement to jar you out of your current thinking pattern. That thinking pattern would have you believe that all self-help books will be full of fluffiness, rainbows, and unicorns and promise the world.

It's called a pattern interrupt.

Now, I would love to know how you responded to that statement when you read it.

There will be people who were angry, people who laughed, people who skimmed over it, people who thought "Good for you, about time someone said it," people who had an "A-ha" moment, people who automatically made excuses, and a whole host of other reactions.

Your reaction will give you an indication of where you are in your life and how strong or weak your ability to respond actually is.

I am not responsible for protecting you and your feelings, which is why I will push you outside your comfort zone, why I will challenge you, and why I will annoy the hell out of you. I have integrity and am honest enough with myself to know that not everyone is going to like what I write, as it means taking full responsibility and not everyone is ready for that yet.

What I am doing by pushing you is showing you your ability to respond, and from this day forward you will tell yourself, *"I Am Responsible for Everything That Happens in My Life."*

What do I mean when I say EVERYTHING that happens in your life?

I mean everything that happens to YOU.

Meaning everything you have active control over. The job you have just now is your responsibility—no excuses, no whining. It is the job you have currently chosen to do. The relationship you're in is your responsibility, the house you live in is your responsibility, your financial situation is your responsibility, and your health is your responsibility.

What Happens When You Take Responsibility?

The first thing that will happen is that you will feel empowered, possibly for the first time in your life.

Where before there were no choices, there suddenly opens up a world of possibilities and choices.

If you hate the job you're in just now, you may feel "I hate this job, I am stuck here, I have no choice but to do this crappy job to pay the bills, and I'm never going to get a better job."

By taking responsibility, you are enabling your ability to respond and saying, "My choices led me to this job, and it will be my choices that lead to a better job."

Can you see how the first thought closes your mind down to possibilities and the second thought opens your mind to possibilities?

Okay, so with the first thought: "I hate this job, I am stuck here, I have no choice but to do this crappy job to pay the bills, and I'm never going to get a better job," your subconscious mind will close down and not look for opportunities in the future, as you have effectively instructed it that there's no point.

Your mind stops looking, stops listening, stops intuiting, and stops feeling for a better job in your life. So you might meet someone at a party who could give you your ideal job, but because you have instructed your subconscious mind to stop looking, it won't recognize the opportunity.

On the other hand, when you take responsibility and instruct your subconscious mind to be on the lookout for better opportunities to get a better job—*"It is my choices that led me to this job, it will be my choices that lead to a better job"*—you will recognize that the person at the party might be someone who can help you find that perfect job.

The first thought instructs your subconscious mind to close down and stop looking for opportunities, while the second thought instructs your mind to open up and be on the lookout for opportunities.

This is an extremely important part of installing this belief, so if you don't quite understand about the closing down and opening up of your subconscious mind, please go back and reread this chapter.

I will give you another example to illustrate this further:

When I first thought about writing a book—I mean a proper book like this one—all kinds of questions and doubts were raised in my mind. I wondered if I really had the expertise, did I have enough to say, would anybody be interested, was it worth my time, who the hell was I to write a book, and a whole host of other questions.

However, the burning desire within me to write this book and share my knowledge was so intense I didn't care if only one person read it as long as I got it out of my mind and wrote the best book I could.

So I affirmed to myself: *"I will write The Belief Principle and attract the people and resources I need to write and market my book."*

That statement above is what kept me going; it is what drove me to keep on writing when I had major doubts. When I was sitting into the wee small hours typing away on yet another edit, telling my wife that it would all be worth it.

Had I given in and thought, "I'm not a writer," my subconscious mind would have shown me all the evidence that I was not a good writer and would have closed down the possibility of even writing this book.

As it happens, my mind expanded and showed me evidence that I could write a book and a good one at that: my passion, my million words written to date on my blog, my knowledge, my research skills, my can-do attitude, my thirst for something new, and a whole batch of evidence to drive and push me to write this.

You see, one direction can close your mind to possibilities, while the other direction opens your mind to possibilities.

I know which direction I would choose every single time.

Now it is time to go and install the belief using the *Deep Soul Feeling Method* described in part three of this book.

Belief No. 3: I Have The Ability To Become Wealthy

"Money is only a tool. It will take you wherever you wish, but it will not replace you as the driver."

AYN RAND

One of the most common self-limiting beliefs is about money and our perceived lack of control over acquiring it.

Would you believe me if I told you that all you need to do to attract more money into your life is to believe you have the ability to become wealthy?

I am not talking about having the skills to bring money into your life; I am simply talking about the belief that you can become wealthy.

Think about it for a few minutes. If you truly believed that there is enough money to go around for everyone—and there is—would that help you feel better about making money?

What if you actually admired wealthy people for their business savvy or their entrepreneurialism, instead of saying things like, "The rich get richer..." "They're probably corrupt," or words to that effect? There are many beliefs that hold us back from having more money in our lives.

Having more money gives us more choices in life. It won't buy you the things that are truly important like happiness, a great family life, true love, passion, knowledge, respect, and inner peace—these things we have to work on separately whether we have money or not. But having more money does give you more choices.

A friend of mine helps clients get higher salaries in their jobs or move to careers with higher salaries, often $30,000-$50,000 per year more.

255

She used to charge $997 for one-on-one coaching for ten sessions. When she expanded her money consciousness and realized her knowledge was worth way more than that, she started charging $6,000, and her client list actually increased as a result.

Your knowledge and your skills are worth so much more than you believe, so isn't it time you expanded your money consciousness?

You've more than likely heard these sayings in your life:

- "Money doesn't grow on trees, you know."
- "We can't afford it."
- "Money can't buy you happiness."
- "The rich get richer and the poor get poorer."
- "To make more money you have to work harder."
- "Money is the root of all evil."

Until you rid yourself of the guilt of trying to better yourself financially, you can't begin to attract more money into your life.

What a lot of people get mixed up with is the difference between greed and making money.

Greed And Money

Regarding some of my heroes, I used to think, "Why would they try and make more money when they obviously don't need it?" I am thinking of people like Richard Branson, James Dyson, Russell Brunson, Jeff Bezos, Warren Buffet, and Tony Robbins, to name but a few.

However, when reading their biographies and watching and listening to interviews, it is clear their goal is not to make more money but to feel alive by building on their brands and their customer loyalty, with the possible exception of Warren Buffet, who is an investment genius.

So their goal is not to make more money—it is a by-product of their goal of achieving more in their lives.

They are also philanthropists, and they give back a hell of a lot to the world in the form of donations, setting up schools, and giving their knowledge and time to the younger generations. This is not greed; it's a desire to reach their potential, which is what Abraham Maslow speaks about in his Hierarchy of Needs theory.

Greed is a different animal altogether. Greed is defined in the *New Oxford English Dictionary* as an "intense and selfish desire for something, especially wealth, power or food."

If your goal is to bring more money into your life simply for your own selfish needs, then life will become empty very quickly.

Giving something back to the world in the form of money, knowledge, education, and time is something everyone should strive for, I believe.

Knowing the difference between greed and money can make a huge difference.

I know in my business, when I stopped focusing on the question "How can I make more money?" and started focusing on the question "How can I help more people?" my business completely turned around, and the money making seemed to come effortlessly.

I also changed my beliefs about money and started to believe it was a lot easier than people imagine.

This is why I include I *Have The Ability To*

The Seven Beliefs That Will Transform Your Life

Become Wealthy in the top seven beliefs that will transform your life.

The conversations and statements of I Will Never Become Wealthy...

- Money doesn't grow on trees.
- I can't afford it.
- Money can't buy you happiness.
- The rich get richer and the poor get poorer.
- To make more money you have to work harder.
- Money is the root of all evil.

The conversations and statements of I Have the Ability to Become Wealthy...

- I am attracting money into my life.
- I always have ideas about how to make more money.
- I always find a way to make money.
- Money is everywhere.
- There is enough money in the world to help everybody.
- I can create wealth in my life.
- I have positive beliefs about money.

The Fiat Principle

Fiat currency is a currency without intrinsic value that has been established as money and is usually backed by the government. This is where the *Fiat Principle* comes into play in our belief systems. We see from the above definition that fiat currency, the pound, the dollar, the euro, the yuan, the peso, etc., are all intrinsically worth nothing, it is only because they are backed by the government that make the pieces of paper they are printed on worth something.

So it is with the *Fiat Principle*. When it comes to work, we have a belief in our minds that we are worth only a certain amount of money per year.

This is often linked to our education, status and relationships.

If I am a doctor, I am apparently worth more money per year than a nurse. You would say that might be right due to the amount of training and responsibility that doctors have compared to nurses.

What about being a member of parliament?

They are paid around £80,000 per year plus expenses for doing what they do. Are they more valuable than firefighters who risk their lives and are paid around £30,000 after becoming qualified?

Again you might say that education comes into play here, but you don't need any qualifications to become a member of parliament, you just need an interest in politics.

So our beliefs about the value of specific careers are forced upon us by other people and when we apply for jobs, we know how much we're going to get, and we tend to think that is all we are worth.

The *Fiat Principle* is something we see in life every single day, but it is rarely acknowledged.

The *Fiat Principle* is a ceiling we have in our minds that limits just how much we are financially worth and affects everything we do from buying clothes to buying homes.

As a child growing up in Edinburgh, I knew from a young age we were relatively poor, and I always felt it. It developed into a kind of snobbishness and resentment of being poor. I remember my mum used to shop at What Every Woman Wants.

I refused to go into the shop with her, and I was only about seven years old. Shopping in WEWW signified to my young mind that we didn't have a lot of money. I am grateful for the clothes and the shoes that my mum and dad bought me from these shops, but I would never be caught dead in them.

This followed me my whole life until I had children and realized you do whatever you can for your kids as long as they are happy, fed, and clothed as best we can afford, and we then shop in places like Primark for ourselves.

However, I started believing that we could bring more money into our lives, I just didn't know how yet. When it started coming in, the *Fiat Principle* came into effect even more.

I had a ceiling, in my mind, of how much I could bring in with my business, and each time I mentally changed that ceiling, I broke through it.

This showed me, for the first time, that we each

have a ceiling, and we all put the fiat principle into action in our lives.

Let me ask you a question now:

Which of these figures makes you feel most uncomfortable, on a scale of one to ten, one being
"that would be really easy" and ten being "no way is that going to happen"?

_____ I could bring in an extra $1,000 this year.
_____ I could bring in an extra $10,000 this year.
_____ I could bring in an extra $25,000 this year.
_____ I could bring in an extra $50,000 this year.
_____ I could bring in an extra $75,000 this year.
_____ I could bring in an extra $100,000 this year.
_____ I could bring in an extra $250,000 this year.
_____ I could bring in an extra $500,000 this year.
_____ I could bring in an extra $1,000,000 this year.

Your ceiling is not the figure you put a ten beside—it is the figure that you scored between a five and a seven on.

A five to seven score would mean it's not easy and it would be a big stretch, but it is possible.

That's a pretty simple exercise, but it is powerful in showing you where your ceiling is.

That's the *Fiat Principle* in action. We put the principle in action when we are looking to buy a house, making an investment, starting a business, buying clothes, looking at our future wealth, and in most other areas of our life where any kind of finances are involved.

Now it is time to go and install the belief using the *Deep Soul Feeling Method* described in part three of this book.

Here's another two amazing things I have done that have made a huge difference in my life and with my relationship with money.

1. Open A New Online Bank Account

Open up a new online bank account, and every single payday transfer one percent of your pay into it. So if you earn $1,000 per month, put $10 into the new account.

As you watch this new account build up over time, you will start to feel differently about money as you know you have the ability to save money and you'll always have money in the bank.

When you have something big you want to buy for yourself or for the family, take it out of this account knowing you don't need debt and feel good about actually saving money first before you buy.

If you want to take it a step further, open up three online bank accounts and label them:

- Treats for myself fund
- Emergency fund
- Big family item fund

Put one percent of your pay into each of the funds every time you get paid. Watch them all build up over time and make a pact with yourself to spend money on yourself every six months or a year. By doing this, you are telling yourself that you are important enough to spend money on, and you won't feel guilty about not spending it on your kids or your family, as you have the other accounts for that.

The other two accounts will be used for those little emergencies that crop up from time to time.

Use the family fund for big items like holidays, kids' school clothes, computers, etc. This is an amazing way to feel wealthy and grow that root belief that you have the ability to become wealthy.

2. Never Pass A Penny On The Street

The other thing I do, which may be a little embarrassing for some people, is to never pass money lying on the street. If it's 5p, 50p, or a 1-pound coin, I will never pass money. When I pick it up, I give a little nod to the universe and thank it for sending me some money.

I have formed the belief that it's the universe's way of sending me little reminders that it has my back, which is why I always thank the universe for sending me money. I also believe I am sending a message to the universe to say I am open to receiving money in my life, and this is a major issue most people have: the inability to be open to receiving money in their lives.

Belief No. 4: I Am Capable Of ANYTHING

"If we did all the things we are capable of

doing, we would literally astound ourselves."

THOMAS A. EDISON

Have you ever said to yourself, or out loud to someone else, "I'm no good at that," "I could never do that," "I wish I could do that," or "You're really talented; it would be great to be able to do that"?

My guess is we've all said that multiple times in our lives. You might not believe this at the moment, but you are literally capable of anything you put your mind to.

Here are a few people who have done just that:

Sir James Dyson. James Dyson made 5,126 attempts at creating the Dyson vacuum cleaner before getting it right. He went through 5,126 prototypes over fifteen years before going on to net his company $4.5 billion.

Thomas Edison. We've all heard the infamous story about Thomas Edison failing 10,000 times with the lightbulb before getting it right.

Apparently in an interview, when asked by a

reporter whether he felt like a failure after so many failed attempts, he said, "I have not failed 10,000 times. I have not failed once. I have succeeded in proving that those 10,000 ways will not work. When I have eliminated the ways that will not work, I will find the way that will work."

Walt Disney. Early on in his career, Walt Disney took a job with the *Kansas City Star*, the local newspaper, but was fired by the editor for lacking imagination and having no good ideas.

He went bankrupt with Laugh-O-Gram Studio, a company that produced short animated cartoons for theatres. In 1923, with the help of his brother Roy, they formed the Disney Brothers Studio, which later became called the Walt Disney Company.

J. K. Rowling. In 1990, at the age of twenty-five, while waiting on a train, the idea for Harry Potter came fully formed to Joanne Kathleen Rowling.

However, it was just a few short months after that her mother, Anne, died from multiple sclerosis, leaving her extremely distraught.

In the wake of her mother's death, she moved to Portugal to teach English. There, she met a man, got married, got pregnant, and gave birth to her daughter, who was born in 1993.

The relationship was a very strenuous one, resulting in divorce. With only three chapters of *Harry Potter and the Philosopher's Stone* completed at the end of 1993, when she was thirty-eight, she moved to Edinburgh, to live with her sister.

In 1995, she eventually finished *Harry Potter and the Philosopher's Stone* and found an agent. The book was rejected by twelve major publishing houses.

Finally in 1996, Bloomsbury gave the green light, and a very small advance of £1,500 was paid. In 1997, seven years after the initial idea, the first *Harry Potter* book was published.

By 2004, Rowling had become the first author to become a billionaire through book writing, according to *Forbes*.

For additional resources, please check the links section.

www.wanderlustworker.com/48-famous-failures-who-will-inspire-you-to-achieve/

What makes the four people mentioned above different from you? Absolutely nothing. The better question would be: what qualities do they have that made them succeed?

The answer is perseverance.

Do you think you could acquire the quality of perseverance? YES is the answer, and you've already got it.

When you were a baby and you first tried to walk, you fell hundreds of times before you succeeded—that's perseverance.

When you were at school and you thought you would never learn your 7 times table before being able to say it without thinking—that's perseverance.

When you first learned to drive and thought you would never be able to do it and then passed your test—that's perseverance.

When you first switched on a computer and

thought you would never get the hang of it, and now you couldn't imagine life without it—that's perseverance.

Those are only some common examples to show that you already have the ability to persevere, and that is all that is required for you to do anything in your life.

You want to learn the piano? Persevere and you will play. You want to be a writer? Persevere and you'll write that book. You want to make more money? Persevere and you'll come across a good idea that makes you money. You want to acquire any skill? Persevere and you'll make it.

I can promise you that if you persevere with anything, you can become proficient at it. I am not going to say you'll write an award-winning book or be able to act on Broadway, but you'll become proficient at anything you put your mind to.

Acquiring the belief of *I Am Capable of Anything* will really set you apart from most people and demonstrating that belief will see you take off in ways you never imagined.

The conversations and statements of I Can't Do That...

- I could never do that.
- I am no good with numbers.
- I am no good with computers.
- I wish I could do what you do.
- If only I could do that.
- I would love to have that ability.
- I've tried a couple of times and couldn't get it.

The conversations and statements of I Am Capable of ANYTHING...

- I am learning more all the time.
- The more I practice, the better I get.
- I love the process of learning something new.
- I'm excited to try it.
- It's tough but I am pushing through it.
- It will all be worth it.

Now it is time to go and install the belief using the *Deep Soul Feeling Method* described in part three of this book.

Belief No. 5: I Am Courageous

"Life shrinks or expands in proportion to one's

courage."

ANAÏS NIN

I was speaking with one of my colleagues from work one day, and she was talking about the fact that she was not good at standing up for herself and hated confrontation.

I asked her if this bothered her, and she confided that it bothered her quite a bit and she wished she could have more courage and stand up for herself.

I then asked if she really wanted to change this aspect of herself, because if she stood up for herself more it would literally change her life.

She gave me a strange look and asked what I meant. I asked her to imagine standing up to all the people she had wanted to in the past and how she would be a different person now. She looked at me and was thinking about what I had said.

She then said it didn't matter, as she has always been like that and shied away from confrontational situations.

I advised her the best thing she could do was to try to involve herself more in confrontational situations.

You can imagine the strange look I received.

Strength Training

We all build up strength by resisting. Think about it for a moment. If you want to build up your body strength, you fight against weights to make your muscles bigger and stronger. If you want to be aerobically fit, you fight against machines to make your lungs stronger. If you want to become smarter, you fight yourself to study and study some more.

Anything we want more of, we have to build up resistance to it. It's just like our bodies fighting a cold—it has to build up its immune system's response to fight the cold.

When I suggested to my colleague that she should involve herself more in confrontational situations, I meant just that.

If she did not walk away from these situations, she would pretty soon become comfortable in them and then learn to stand up for herself more.

You can also do this with all aspects of your life. To be more courageous, put yourself in more situations that require courage.

To be able to stand up for yourself more, put yourself in more situations where you will have to stand up for yourself. This way you build up a resistance to the stress you may feel in these situations.

To be a better speaker, put yourself in situations where you will have to speak more.

Having the belief that you are courageous will change your life in ways you can't even fathom just now.

Imagine you are in a situation where you need courage to speak out or stand up for yourself. Your old self might tell you to "stay silent and don't stand up."

However, when you have the deep belief that you are courageous, then that will give you the strength to stand up and speak out.

The Belief Principle

Even if you're nervous, even if you get tongue-tied, even if you think people will laugh at you.

The more you do this, the more courageous you will become.

The conversations and statements of I Don't Have The Courage For That...

- I hate confrontation.
- I'm not good at standing up for myself.
- I wish I could be more assertive.
- I wish I had the courage to do that.
- It would be great to chase my dream, but...
- I'm too scared to do that.
- What if they laugh at me?
- What if it doesn't work out?

The conversations and statements of I Am Courageous...

- I was scared, but I had to go for it I'm so glad I got over my fear.
- I feel an inner power.
- I am way outside my comfort zone, but it feels good I am constantly growing as a person.
- I love to try different things.
- I feel so much more confident.

- I don't take shit from anybody.
- I know my worth.

Now it is time to go and install the belief using the *Deep Soul Feeling Method* described in part three of this book.

Belief No. 6: I Never Settle For Second Best

> *"The minute you settle for less than you deserve, you get even less than you settled for."*

MAUREEN DOWD

Do you know what you want from life?

Most of us know what we'd love to have in our lives but often feel that what we'd love is just out of reach. So we dream about those things.

However, very few of us sit down and really think about what we realistically want in our lives. That includes our work, our love lives, our passions, our dreams, our spirituality, and our goals.

When you can really sit down and think about what you'd like to have in your life, you will find that what you'd like is within your grasp—you just haven't taken the time to ask yourself what it is you really want.

Instead, what a lot of us do is settle. We settle for a mediocre love life, we settle for a shitty job, we settle for our friends, we settle for the clothes we wear, we settle for the goals we chase…you get the picture here.

What settling means is that you get comfortable. You sit on the sofa inside your comfort zone and say, "It's comfy here, it's not too difficult, and there's not much effort involved."

And that's okay if you've thought about it and you're happy sitting on the sofa inside your comfort zone.

What generally happens, though, is that we say, "It's comfy here, it's not too difficult, and there's not much effort involved, but I am not happy."

And that's because we're settling for second best.

Sometimes we don't quite know why we're unhappy, we just know we are. The answer to this problem is knowing what you want in the different areas of your life and being courageous enough, having enough confidence, and knowing you are worthy enough to never ever settle for second best.

My wife and I recently wanted to move to a new house to downsize after our grown children had flown the nest and my wife's father had passed away.

We knew the exact type of place we wanted. We wanted to live in one of the old tenement-style apartments in the West End of Glasgow. You heard the rest of that story already—we decided not to settle, and we eventually found the right property, the right financial advisor, the right mortgage, and the right price to get the apartment we wanted. And we absolutely love it. We love it all the more because we didn't settle for second best.

There is a beautiful line in the book, *The Perks of Being a Wallflower* by Stephen Chbosky which perfectly illustrates what I am talking about here.

The scene in the book is when Charlie, the main character, asks his English teacher, "Why do nice people pick the wrong people to date?"

After thinking about it for a few seconds, his English teacher replies, "We accept the love we think we deserve."

There is more in that one line that sums up the human psyche than a four-year degree course in psychology will teach you.

It's exactly the same in life: We accept the life we think we deserve.

If you think you deserve mediocrity, you will only ever achieve mediocrity. It's only when you start to believe that you deserve more in life that you will rise higher and overcome the obstacles and rise to higher places.

This goes for every single area of your life.

I'd like you to do something right now. Think about these eight areas of your life:

1. Romantic love.
2. Family and friends.

3. Passions.
4. Health.
5. Money.
6. Career.
7. Spirituality.
8. Outcomes (goals).

As you think about each area, ask yourself this one question:

Am I settling for second best?

The answer will be instinctual, so go with your first answer without feeling guilt and without thinking about it too much.

When you've done that, I would like you to say out loud:

"I NEVER settle for second best!"

The conversations and statements of I Don't Deserve More…

- There's no point in trying for that.
- People like me never get…
- I can't afford the dress/suit I really want so I will get this one.

- I'd love someone to truly see me but that's just a dream, so I'll make the most of this relationship.
- This is not my ideal career but it's okay and it pays well.
- I'd love to be a writer but that's just a pipe dream.
- I'd love to be slimmer but I'm okay with the way I am.

The conversations and statements of I Never Settle For Second Best...

- I can't afford what I want right now so I'll wait until I can get what I want.
- My partner doesn't treat me right and I am not settling for anything less than a great relationship so they're out.
- In order to build myself a better future, I can do without some luxuries.
- If I don't like something, I won't do it.
- I don't have the career I'd love so I will attend more training at night school until I can switch careers.
- I have set healthy boundaries in all my relationships and I expect to be treated with respect.

- I don't waste my time gathering friends, I nurture the friendships I already have.

Now it is time to go and install the belief using the *Deep Soul Feeling Method* described in part three of this book.

Belief No. 7: I AM Enough

"The feeling that 'I am enough' does not mean that I have nothing to learn, nothing further to achieve, and nowhere to grow to. It means that I accept myself, that I am not on trial in my own eyes, that I value and respect myself. This is not an act of indulgence but of courage."

NATHANIEL BRANDEN

So many people today do not view themselves as being enough. They constantly berate themselves, and gauge themselves based on what other people are doing.

Social media has exacerbated this; however, we cannot blame social media as I see social media being used as a huge tool for growth, but it is up to us how we use it.

We've all had that feeling of not being good enough somehow and it manifests itself in many different ways. I have heard people say, "I am not thin enough to go to the gym."

People who want to lose weight would feel far too vulnerable should they go to the gym because they are overweight. Imagine going to the gym and feeling so self conscious about your weight that you couldn't get on with the exercise at hand.

That has all to do with belief and it's such a shame, and partly the reason I wrote this book.

We are living in a world where we just don't feel enough for whatever reason. What we're really trying to do is fit in.

We are born with an inherent need to fit in, to belong to a tribe and when we are brave enough to try and join a new tribe that's when our vulnerabilities come out, that's where the phrase "I am not enough" manifests itself.

I know I don't know you yet, but I know for sure that you are enough, you are brave, you are strong, you are smart, and you make a difference.

When you make a difference, then you are enough.

This last belief of the book is so vitally important to understand and install for everyone.

Younger people are extremely vulnerable and susceptible to having the feeling that they are not enough as they live and breath social media, whether that be through YouTube, Facebook, Instagram, TikTok, or Snapchat.

The new "superstars" of today are self made and have come from social media. Young people today are asking "What is different about them? Why am I not enough?"

As for the older generation, well, we've always been a little screwed up and it's time to stop that cycle.

The conversations and statements of I Am Not Enough...

- I am not thin enough.
- I am not intelligent enough.
- I am not social enough.
- I don't earn enough.

- I am not funny enough.
- I am not good looking.
- I can't show my true self in front of others.

The conversations and statements of I Am Enough...

- I am what I am.
- I am not perfect but that doesn't matter.
- I am scared but I am going to do it.
- I feel vulnerable but I know it is worth it.
- I am worthy.
- I can let go and be myself.
- I enjoy my own company.

Now, it is time to go and install the belief using the *Deep Soul Feeling Method* described in part three of this book.

USING THE BELIEF PRINCIPLES

In Other Areas Of Your Life

Belief Principle For Business Leaders

"Become the kind of leader that people would follow voluntarily; even if you had no title or position."

BRIAN TRACY

I will be adding a bonus chapter on this in the resources section of the membership site at *www.TheBeliefPrinciple.com/resources.*

Belief Principle For Entrepreneurs

"Every time you state what you want or believe, you're the first to hear it. It's a message to both you and others about what you think is possible.

Don't put a ceiling on yourself."

OPRAH WINFREY

I will be adding a bonus chapter on this in the resources section of the membership site at: *www.TheBeliefPrinciple.com/resources.*

Belief Principle For Parents

"Your kids require you most of all to love them for who they are, not to spend your whole time trying to correct them."

BILL AYERS

I will be adding a bonus chapter on this in the resources section of the membership site at: *www.TheBeliefPrinciple.com/resources.*

Belief Principle For Writers

"You can always edit a bad page. You can't edit a blank page."

JODI PICOULT

I will be adding a bonus chapter on this in the resources section of the membership site at:

www.TheBeliefPrinciple.com/resources.

Belief Principle For Salespeople

"Everything you've ever wanted is on the other side of fear."

GEORGE ADAIR

I will be adding a bonus chapter on this in the resources section of the membership site at: *www.TheBeliefPrinciple.com/resources.*

Belief Principle For Teens

"Stop trying to be less of who you are. Let this time in your life cut you open and drain all of the things that are holding you back."

JENNIFER ELISABETH

I will be adding a bonus chapter on this in the resources section of the membership site at: *www.TheBeliefPrinciple.com/resources.*

Belief Principle For Traders

"What seems too high and risky to the

majority generally goes higher and what seems low and cheap generally goes lower."

WILLIAM O'NEIL

I will be adding a bonus chapter on this in the resources section of the membership site at: *www.TheBeliefPrinciple.com/resources*.

Belief Principle For Couples

"The best and most beautiful things in the world cannot be seen or even heard but must be felt with the heart."

HELEN KELLER

I will be adding a bonus chapter on this in the resources section of the membership site at: *www.TheBeliefPrinciple.com/resources*.

Belief Principle For Recovering From Addiction

"If there's one thing I learned in Al-Anon, it's that you got to face the music because it just grows louder when you ignore it."

VICKI COVINGTON

Using The Belief Principles

I will be adding a bonus chapter on this in the resources section of the membership site at: *www.TheBeliefPrinciple.com/resources*.

The Belief Principle

CONCLUSION

The True Purpose Of Changing Your Beliefs

Most people go to their grave not knowing what their true purpose was in life and for me that's quite sad. It means that most people just get by by being alive and not feeling truly enthused with their life.

Imagine your life if you were to wake up every morning really excited to jump out of bed and ready to start the day. The reason you jump out of bed is that you know you are making a difference in someone's life. You may not know them, but you are making a difference.

I have spoken to thousands of people during my coaching, in my business life, in seminars, and just talking to friends and family. That's why I feel confident in saying that most people don't truly know what they want out of their life.

We all know what we don't want but we haven't a clue as to what we truly want. When I say knowing what you want in life, I don't mean for you to say, "Oh I would love to be sitting on a beach reading all day."

That is not a life, that is a holiday. I mean finding your true purpose.

Once you've installed the seven major beliefs, you'll have the confidence, the courage, and the determination to become wealthy. Once you have all that, what is next?

Well, a lot of people would love to have even a fraction of what these beliefs will bring you and they might be extremely happy with their life. However, a lot more people will find the next level in their evolution to be a lot more exciting.

So, what is the next level?

Well, I can't tell you what it will be for you, but I know what it will be for a lot of people: It's being of service to others.

Now I don't mean in a holier-than-thou kind of way.

Conclusion

I mean you might find that you need to share with others what you have learned or that you want to help humanity in a much more meaningful way. This can be done in many different ways such as through writing, teaching, speaking, creating courses, creating seminars and a plethora of other ways. The point is your energy and consciousness will be raised to another level so much so that you will start to see life in a different way, in a much more meaningful way.

You see, by changing your beliefs you will change your whole energy. Your aura will literally change, and you will be vibrating at a different level than what you were before.

When you realize that finding your purpose will be your next quest, your life becomes so much more exciting and you'll see it as a turning point in your life.

I hope this book has helped you see yourself in a different way and helped you to realize that there is so much more to life than you first imagined. This is only a few steps on the journey of life, and I am glad you decided to share this part of your journey with me.

Hopefully, you've found this book worthwhile and you can see the benefits of carrying out the exercises I mentioned earlier.

A lot of people don't want to do the exercises enclosed to make lasting change, so I want to make it easier on you:

Just do one thing every day. Honestly, if you literally just take 15 minutes per day and listen to the deep soul feeling mantra, you will see a huge difference this time next year. Of course if you want to ramp it up, then make time for the other exercises as you will change at a much quicker rate.

You will see subtle changes, like feeling more confident, feeling a little more sociable or start to believe in yourself more and feel more assertive. That is just one of the beliefs mentioned. There are literally hundreds of beliefs you may want to install, but I would try and stick with root beliefs right now as these are the ones that will have the most impact.

Please do join the Facebook group as well to get support: *www.TheBeliefPrinciple.com/group.*

Join the Telegram group which is more instant and not as restricted as Facebook at:
www.TheBeliefPrinciple.com/telegram

Also download all the MP3's I have prepared to go along with this book and other goodies at:
www.TheBeliefPrinciple/resources

You can also join our monthly program where you get a new set of affirmations every month along with training and live videos.
www.TheBeliefPrinciple.com/store.

Links

- Free Resources:
  www.thebeliefprinciple.com/resources
- Exclusive Facebook group:
  www.thebeliefprinciple.com/FBGroup
- Belief Principle Store:
  www.TheBeliefPrinciple.com/store
- The Telegram Group:
  www.TheBeliefPrinciple.com/telegram

Please leave a review of the book...

I would be forever grateful if you could leave a review of this book on Amazon. You might not know it, but your review is really valuable and can help other people to find the book and you are helping to change someone else's life in the process.

Of course, if you hated the book, then please let me know with a review as well. I've got big broad Scottish shoulders so I can handle the bad reviews as well as the good reviews.

ABOUT THE AUTHOR

Steven Aitchison is an author, speaker, and online trainer.

Self Improvement

He teaches self improvement focusing on beliefs and self worth.

You can check out his website *www.stevenaitchison.co.uk* for hundreds of free articles and videos.

Business

Steven has taught hundreds of people around the world how to grow their business using social media.

You can check out his *Your Digital Formula* program at: *www.YourDigitalFormula.com*.

Social Media Links

Website: *www.stevenaitchison.co.uk*

Self-Improvement Store:
www.TheBeliefPrinciple.com/store

🅕 *www.facebook.com/changeyourthoughtstoday*

🅞 *www.instagram.com/stevenpaitchison*

🅣 *www.twitter.com/stevenaitchison*

🅘 *www.linkedin.com/in/stevenaitchison*

Contact

To contact Steven, please use the email address: steven@thebeliefprinciple.com.

Made in the USA
Columbia, SC
05 July 2021

41416634R00170